Literacy

as a human problem

Litər

acy

as a human problem

edited by JAMES C. RAYMOND

THE UNIVERSITY OF ALABAMA PRESS
University, Alabama

Library of Congress Cataloging in Publication Data

Main entry under title:

Literacy as a human problem.

Papers presented at the 6th Alabama Symposium on English and
American Literature held at the University of Alabama in 1979.
Includes bibliographies and index.
1. Illiteracy—Congresses. 2. English language—Study and teaching—
Congresses. I. Raymond, James C., 1940–   . II. Alabama Symposium on
English and American Literature (6th : 1979 : University of Alabama)
LC149.L498   428.2'07'073   81-19757
ISBN 0-8173-0108-9 (cloth)   AACR2
ISBN 0-8173-0110-0 (paper)

Contents

In Memory of Mina

Acknowledgments

These essays were first read as papers in a symposium on literacy conducted at The University of Alabama. Thanks to the generosity of the speakers, including two—E. D. Hirsch and James Sledd—who are regrettably not represented in this volume, the symposium was an unqualified success. Widely divergent points of view remained widely divergent, and few, if any, minds were changed; but the speakers performed admirably, and the audience, which had come from thirty-seven states, seemed to feel that each viewpoint had been expressed as articulately and persuasively as anyone could express it.

I am deeply grateful to The University of Alabama for making the symposium and this publication possible. I am particularly grateful to the former president, David Mathews, the former academic vice-president, Richard Thigpen, Dean Douglas E. Jones, and Dean William B. Bryan, all of whom committed funds from their budgets to support the symposium. I am equally grateful to the Committee for Humanities in Alabama, which matched the University's contributions with a munificent grant. I am also grateful to my colleagues in the English Department, who generously supported literacy as a topic in a symposium series that had been the exclusive preserve of literary topics, and to Carol McGinnis Kay, then chairwoman of the department, and to Claudia Johnson, her successor, for supporting the symposium series and for providing the released time I needed to edit the papers. I am especially grateful to the contributors themselves, who spent three days on our campus igniting discussions that may make us more cautious and less doctrinaire in

our deliberations about literacy and its human consequences.

Finally, I should like to acknowledge a debt to Mina P.
Shaughnessy, who brought to the teaching of writing an
uncommon combination of scholarship, insight, and compassion. It was Mina who suggested the title of the symposium, and it is to her memory that the collection is
dedicated.

The University of Alabama   JAMES C. RAYMOND

Literacy

as a human problem

Introduction: Literacy as a Human Problem

Leonard Bloomfield, one of the first scientific linguists in America, claimed that writing was not language at all, but "merely a way of recording language by means of visible marks."[1] Bloomfield's notion that ordinary spoken language is a fit subject for scientific study—more fit, indeed, than printed English—was a radical departure from the tradition in which English as it was used by careful writers was considered the norm, and varieties of spoken English were regarded as deviations or corruptions. And though this new perspective is now axiomatic in the fields of dialectology, sociolinguistics, and theoretical grammar, its application to lexicography and to the teaching of composition is still a matter of considerable controversy. The controversy is growing old, but as this volume will show, no less lively. It has spread from scholars and journalists to include parents, schoolteachers, legislators, and the courts.

If the essays seem disparate, it is because the collection is not limited to a single viewpoint or methodology. It includes journalists as well as academicians, and among the academicians, some who are more interested in the applications of scholarship and others who are more interested in theory or in the interpretation of historical data. In this respect the collection reflects the range of the controversy, a range that is both valuable and inevitable. To understand the nature of literacy, its benefits, and its often unperceived costs, we will have to take each perspective on its own terms, not expecting the journalist to provide references or case studies and not allowing the scholar to do without them.

The essays cover three major issues: Part One deals with the controversy over standard English and minority dialects; Part Two deals with the controversy over testing; and Part Three deals with the nature of literacy itself, about which there has been too little controversy because there have been too few serious studies. In general the essays tend to be more scholarly as they move from debates about practice to speculations about theory. But if history repeats itself, speculations like those offered by Walter Ong in the last chapter will enrich the quality of public debate, just as Bloomfield's speculations, addressed mainly to other scholars nearly fifty years ago, eventually unsettled public opinions that seemed to be firmly rooted in common sense.

Taken together, the essays illustrate one of the most puzzling paradoxes in contemporary education: the inability of literate people to agree about the nature and value of literacy. It would be no surprise if the disagreement were confined to extremists of one kind or another—social snobs or political demagogues. But it is not. It defies established lines of demarcation, polarizing reasonable people of every stripe. It makes fast allies of individuals who might agree on no other political, social, or economic policy. Like any genuinely complex disagreement in which human values are at stake, it provokes debates and discussions that are rarely dispassionate and never conclusive. If this were merely a debate about scholarly esoterica, the public could afford to wait it out. But the consequences of this debate are immediate and widespread. No problem in American education today is more urgent than teaching children how to read and write.

On one level, the disagreement about literacy is a clash between two distinct ways of reacting to language, each respectable in itself. We may react to language as linguistic scientists, like Bloomfield, or we may react to it as participants. When we react to it as scientists we insist upon empirical data, and we refuse to make value judgments about right and wrong, about elegance or inelegance. Scientists are supposed to describe what they observe; they are not expected to tell us how they like what they observe or what they wish they had observed. When we react to language as participants, we indulge in value judgments colored by expectations and sensibilities developed over a lifetime of listening and reading. We generally prefer the variety of language that we consider "normal," though for each of us the perception of normality has been biased by our linguistic experiences (or lack thereof) at home, in school, and on paper.

Neither perspective is superior to the other. The trick is to use each when it is appropriate—to look at language scientifically when we want to make statements that should be empirically justified, and to look at it phenomenologically when we want to say how various words, phrases, styles, or dialects strike us as participants and how they are likely to strike other participants.

As it happens, people seem unable or unwilling to switch from one perspective to the other when it would be appropriate to do so. Linguists prefer the scientific perspective, and they tend to regard other observers as amateurs and dilettantes. Linguists are committed to gathering and explaining data; they have no professional interest in value judgments about the language they observe because value judgments are alien to the methodology of science. Journalists, editors, and other educated writers, however, thrive on discriminations between what they perceive to be right and wrong, better and worse, basing these judgments upon logical distinctions, upon etymological records, upon analogies in foreign languages (particularly Latin), and even upon thoroughly subjective impressions of euphony. Judgments of this sort may not be scientific, but they are not for that reason immoral: professional writers and editors have no real choice except to view language from the perspective of participants, in deference to the expectations of other participants. To them, the linguists' refusal to judge quality is a denial of the phenomenology of language, a denial of common sense. Like blind men groping at different parts of an elephant, linguists cling to the data of language as if there were no phenomenology, while writers and editors cling to the phenomenology without consulting the data, each side claiming to have the only purchase on the truth.

It is in this context that debates like the one represented in this book are possible. When John Simon warns that the deterioration of our language may soon require us to ask "for who the bell tolls," he is speaking with the sensibilities of a stylist and a journalist, and the audience responds with sympathetic laughter. Linguists, however, cringe at Simon's ostensible disregard of the evolutionary forces that have been stripping inflections from English nouns and pronouns for centuries without detriment to the language.

Conversely, when linguists speak about language as if all its varieties were inherently equal, they make sense only to other linguists. Thus when Elisabeth McPherson says that her first step in teaching in a community college was to tell her students they were already "experts in the essentials of English grammar," the linguists in the audience may applaud. Journalists, however, and other interested nonlinguists will shake their heads in disbelief. Even if they understand that McPherson uses the word *grammar* in a technical sense defined by other linguists, their instincts tell them *that's not the sort of grammar teachers are paid to teach. If you are going to tell students that they already know what they need to know, there is no point in our sending them to school.* McPherson, of course, does teach skills in the classroom, and Simon does know something about the history of the language; but their positions tend to be polarized in debate.

In political confrontations between a far left and a far right, there is usually a middle ground where we can find, if not justice and truth, at least expedience. In this debate, there is no middle ground. To be tolerant at some times and rigorous at others is not a reasonable position; it is no position at all. If we ignore the social and scientific data about language, we will systematically alienate millions of children whose linguistic heritage happens to be different from the tradition hallowed by editors, academicians, and professional writers. If we ignore the aesthetic dimensions of language, we will undermine our respect for craftsmanship, precision, and beauty in writing—all of which, presumably, should be fostered in the schools.

The problem is that linguists and traditionalists do not have extreme points of view. Their points of view are simply different, just as art and anatomy are different perspectives on the human body. The "truth" is not some sort of compromise between the two; it is, to the extent that it is knowable at all, a composite of the two, and of other perspectives as well.

When they are playing to friendly audiences, traditionalists and linguists can each choose to disdain the other's perspectives. In shaping policies and pedagogies for schools, however, we need them both. Teachers need to think like linguists when they want to make factual determinations about language. If the language students bring with them to the classroom happens to differ from the language in the textbooks (and to some extent it always does), teachers cannot deal with it intelligently without first understanding some basic linguistic facts: that the differences among dialects are differences, not corruptions; that usage is a matter of convention, not a constraint of logic; that the aesthetics of usage are culturally and historically relative, not rooted in absolute norms; and that each variety of English has a grammatical system of its own that is neither more nor less valid than any other. These are hard insights for people who have not studied language with the disinterested rationality of scientists. Admitting these facts about language does not absolve teachers from their responsibility to teach the sort of writing that has been normalized in print. But it is not likely that they will develop humane and effective pedagogies without first acknowledging the facts for what they are.

Nor is it likely that teachers will develop effective pedagogies if they are not themselves good writers and editors. Traditionally we have assumed that schoolteachers knew their "grammar" and that they were equipped to police the borders of usage. It is no longer safe to make these assumptions. Many teachers in classrooms today have been trained in theoretical linguistics, but not in the sort of grammar and usage that editors apply. Many are products of colleges of education in which tolerance of dialectal diversity has degenerated to a total disregard for the conventions of literacy. The result, predictably enough, is that teachers are often insecure as writers and editors, and that the guidance they give their pupils is chancy at best. Perhaps now, after the dramatic failure of various structural and transformational grammars in the schools (where they were expected to produce effects they were not designed to produce), we may realize that the difference between linguists and editors is analogous to the difference between theoreticians and practitioners in any field. In effect, proper training for English teachers might reasonably include healthy doses of writing and editing courses in addition to courses that view language from the value-free perspective of linguists.

Perhaps the most spectacular impasse between the scientists and the practitioners of language is the refusal of each to recognize that the other has something valid to say about the existence and nature of standard English. The practitioners feel in their bones that there must be some logical, historical, or metaphysical basis for what they perceive to be the difference between right and wrong usage. They treat linguistic data to the contrary as an archbishop might treat a heretical scientist: if science cannot verify what we already know to be true, then it is the science that is at fault, not the truth.

Linguists, on the other hand, disdain the refusal of the practitioners to face facts and are suspicious of the practitioners' motives for doing so. The facts are beyond controversy. The notion that there is an oral American standard in any meaningful sense has been discredited by the field work of dialectologists, whose data, now emerging as a series of linguistic atlases of the United States, show remarkable differences in spoken English even among educated Americans. These data might be easily corroborated by any amateur linguist who would walk with attentive ears through the streets of Brooklyn, Charleston, New Orleans, Los Angeles, Martha's Vineyard, Tuskegee, Opelousas, or Sante Fe.

There is conceivably a written standard English—or "edited American English" as it is called in the resolution entitled "The Students' Right to Their Own Language"—in the sense that some locutions and conventions are statistically more likely to appear in edited English than others, except when the writer is deliberately affecting the idiom of speech. Linguistic data, however, and common sense suggest that only a perilously small minority of Americans, including those with diplomas of one kind or another, can or ever could produce English fit for print without the assistance of an editor, and that few, if any of us, restrict our speech to the sort of English that editors approve. To admit these facts is to admit that standard English, if it exists at all, is a minority dialect. The world of high literacy in this country is not a huge melting pot in which all but a few recalcitrant minorities have been purified of their linguistic quirks. It is a relatively small teakettle with a very powerful whistle. Few people outside of English departments and publishing houses know what that teakettle looks like from the inside. To make mastery of standard English an educational or occupational requirement (except in professions where mastery is what lawyers call a "bona fide occupational qualification") is not only an act of faith in possibilities that no culture in history has ever achieved; it is, in its actual effect, a form of cultural and linguistic aggression, if not genocide. On the other hand, to abandon the conventions—to give up the efficiency of normalization or the pleasure of style—is an act of cultural irresponsibility, if not suicide.

It is tempting to avoid the problem of dialectal pluralism by prescinding from the surface features of language and considering writing, as D'Angelo does in his review of Luria's work, from a third perspective, the perspective of cognitive psychology, from which literacy is seen not as a style of language but as a style of thought. What D'Angelo and Luria have to say on this matter is largely consistent with one of Walter Ong's most intriguing themes: that literacy, like any other medium, alters the noetic habits of the people who acquire it—that is, it alters the way people think. With Havelock, Perry, Lord, and other scholars cited in his work, Ong argues that literate cultures (e.g., the Greece of Aristotle) tend to think differently from oral cultures, even highly developed oral cultures (e.g., the Greece of Homer). The oral culture could produce and preserve the *Iliad*, but not the *Metaphysics;* and the literate culture that made the *Metaphysics* possible also made the old oral traditions obsolete. From this perspective the battle over apostrophes and inflections seems petty. And in the case of the Greeks, it is fairly obvious that over the course of history, the benefits of literacy—the tradition of literature, scholarship, law, and technology that literacy made possible—were commensurate with the costs.

The sociology of literacy presents different problems, however, when it involves literate and nonliterate peoples living in the same political and economic systems. In these circumstances, the acquisition of literacy is not experienced as a cultural evolution in which everyone participates, but rather as a conflict between two cultures, each of which perceives the other as a threat. The predictable hostilities are exacerbated when the two cultures are also split along ethnic or religious lines, even when the literate culture chooses to insist that the nonliterate group acquire the benefits of literacy. The Soviet attempt to save the Uzbeks from their own traditions is a painful case in point. When Luria and his colleagues examined the causes and effects of literacy in Uzbekistan, their motives were doubtlessly benign: they wanted to improve the economic conditions of the Uzbeks and to disprove the notion that backward cultures are caused by ethnic or genetic deficiencies. But to achieve these ends, the Soviets considered it necessary to destroy the Moslem culture in the process, replacing it with the technology and the political consciousness of a literate culture. Luria expresses his disdain for Islam candidly:

Despite the high levels of creativity in science, art, and architecture attained in the ancient culture of Uzbekistan, the masses had lived for centuries in economic stagnation and illiteracy, their development hindered among other things by the religion of Islam. Only the radical restructuring of the economy, the rapid elimination of illiteracy, and the removal of the Moslem influence could achieve, over and above an expansion in the world view, a genuine revolution in cognitive activity.[2]

In other words, literacy was one weapon among several used by the Soviets to wipe out an old order and establish not only technology, but political and cognitive orthodoxy, with no effort to restore the humanistic accomplishments that the Uzbeks had once achieved on their own and with no attention to the traditions of literature and critical thinking that had accrued to the Greeks when literacy evolved among them spontaneously. Luria's description of the freedom literacy would engender seems less than liberating in its details:

When the socialist revolution eliminated dominance and submission as class relations, people oppressed one day enjoyed a free existence the next. . . . The appearance of a new economic system brought with it new forms of social activity: the collective evaluation of work plans, the recognition and correction of shortcomings, and the allocation of economic functions. Naturally the socioeconomic life of these regions underwent a complete transformation. The radical changes in social class structure were accompanied by cultural shifts.[3]

Whether the Soviets actually achieved their objectives is a moot question. No one doubts the cognitive changes that Luria attributes to the acquisition of literacy, though we do not know whether these changes had the effects on culture, politics, and economy that he predicted. Writing forty years after the project, Luria himself claimed that the people of Uzbekistan had "made a leap of centuries" so obvious to any observer that to repeat his research at this time "would be superfluous."[4] If, indeed, the Soviets did improve the material and political conditions of the Uzbeks, the Islamic culture seems to have survived the process: figures published recently in the *Atlantic* (January 1981) indicate that the population of Uzbekistan is still between 80 and 90 percent Moslem.

The obvious lesson of Luria's research is that literacy alters the consciousness of individuals who acquire it. The less obvious lessons, apparently, are that literacy is a powerful engine of politics, that its effects can be regarded as liberation or enslavement, depending upon how we regard the system that employs it, and that forcing literacy upon a hapless people can be an act of aggression just as brutal as denying literacy in the name of order and stability.

The closer we get to home, the more difficult it is to see literacy from this fourth perspective, the perspective of sociology. It is relatively easy for people in the United States to regard the illiterate campesinos of Central America as victims of unequal schooling rather than as moral or genetic failures; it is much more difficult for us to regard minorities in our own country with the same compassion. We assume that anyone with sufficient character and intelligence ought to be able, with the help of the local public school, to make the "leap of centuries" Luria described.

The sociology of literacy is almost exactly analogous to the sociology of wealth. Success depends upon a fortuitous combination of circumstance and effort. Given extremely favorable circumstances, success is almost inevitable; given extremely unfavorable circumstances, failure is virtually certain. And in both realms—literacy and economics—success, failure, and even mediocrity each have an inertia that spans generations. To compli-

cate matters, the inertia of success and the inertia of
failure often run along ethnic lines, reinforced by cultural predilections as well as by traditional or legal barriers.

Literacy, then, despite its advantages, is a human
problem in much the same way that wealth is. It is,
ironically, the condition that makes illiteracy possible,
just as wealth makes poverty possible. Like wealth, literacy can divide civilizations into hostile factions, the
haves and the have-nots. And like wealth, literacy is a
problem not only to those who lack it, but often to those
who have it as well. Neither wealth nor literacy guaran-
tees superior sensibility; either can engender a warped
set of values, fashionable vulgarity, and callousness toward the disadvantaged. People who are highly literate,
like people who are very rich, are tempted to regard
literacy or money as the measure of human worth. There
are no easy solutions to either problem. The poor will
always be with us; literacy will never be universal.

"The true test of civilization," Samuel Johnson is re-
puted to have said, is "a decent provision for the poor."
Progressive governments around the world are generally
committed to the notion that decent provisions should be
made, not only that the poor might survive, but that with
a reasonable amount of effort they might become self-
sufficient. "Decent," however, is not an objective measure, and the core of political debate everywhere is the
attempt to determine the extent to which government
ought to intervene to break cycles of failure. People who
believe that effort, more than circumstance, accounts for
success belong to the party on the right; people who
believe that circumstance, more than effort, accounts for
failure belong to the party on the left. Because effort is by
definition self-conscious and circumstance is generally
taken for granted, successful people tend to be more

aware of the efforts that got them where they are than of the circumstances that made their efforts flourish. Extremists at either end of the political spectrum are people who more or less completely deny the role either of effort or of circumstance.

In the debate about literacy, the sociological perspective makes odd bedfellows with the other three perspectives (linguistics, phenomenology, and cognitive psychology). In general, people who regard themselves as accomplished writers know full well that writing is hard work, and they tend to value effort more than circumstance. Even those whose politics are progressive in other ways find it difficult to understand why a nonliterate environment cannot be overcome by individual diligence. But people who have studied language and language acquisition from a scientific perspective tend to be more aware of the tyranny of circumstance. For them, the conditions under which language is learned are such powerful determinants of performance that the only logical policies seem to be either radical tolerance of diversity or radical intervention to prevent it. Accomplished writers who understand the scientific perspective on literacy are anomalous creatures, like wealthy progressives, ostensibly opposed to their own interests.

In human terms, the relationship between effort and circumstance is illustrated by a group of first graders who are holding books in their hands for the first time in their lives, while in the next classroom a second group can already recognize letters and a few words in print. Even if intensive instruction can bridge the difference between these two groups in the early years, the breach will reappear in the third grade or the fourth, when the texts explode with thousands of vocabulary items that only one group will have heard or seen at home. At this point, the standardized test scores will distinguish the haves from the have-nots as surely as their parents' tax returns.

And at the college level, how do we tell the unfit from the untrained? How do we distinguish the bright freshman who has never been taught to read and write from the freshman who would not have learned under any circumstances? When we can identify the bright and willing in this group, are we justified in leading them to believe that anything short of heroic effort and extraordinary luck will make them skillful readers and mature writers? Is it kindness or cruelty to invite them all to attempt a "leap of centuries," thereby implying that it is their own fault if they fail?

It would be convenient if literacy could be given out like hot lunches in the schools—cultural nourishment to make avid readers of children who see no books at home. It would be convenient if dialects, like suits of clothes, existed independently of the people who use them, so that we could distribute more fashionable linguistic habits to needy children as charitably and inconspicuously as we give them good shoes and warm jackets. But although all children can switch registers at will, speaking colloquially or formally to suit the occasion, and although some of them can mimic regional or alien accents to perfection, there is no evidence that children in general can learn to love books or change linguistic habits deeply ingrained at home by spending a few hours a day in even the most enlightened and supportive of classrooms. Occasionally we hear of individual teachers or particular programs that seem reasonably or even spectacularly successful. But no one has yet developed a formula that can be packaged and distributed. Successful writing programs succeed because of a fortuitous match-up of personalities and values: take away the ambitions of a certain group of pupils or the support of their parents, and the program fails; take away the energy, enthusiasm, and insight of a certain teacher, and the program also fails.

Mina Shaughnessy, to whom this book is dedicated, was one such teacher. Anyone who knew her well knows that she was even more extraordinary than the book she left us. She was an elegant writer and a graceful person, patient, courageous, creative, scholarly, and wise. As director of the writing program at City College when it opened its doors to every high school graduate in Harlem, Mina tolerated no illusions about the odds against success. She was a realist. But she was not content with the reality she saw, and she persuaded those who heard her at City and elsewhere that the odds could be changed, if only we would match the effort required of our students with heroic efforts of our own. She explored chasms of the mind that most of us feared, and she persuaded us that the view there was not dangerous, not hostile, and not without its beauty. Her ability to perceive the human value of the students she worked with was perhaps her most impressive quality, a fifth perspective on literacy, all the more powerful because she had not neglected to become expert in the other four. It is hard to say whether Mina moved us more with her insight or with her affection. Both made us, like her students, believe we could succeed. Both will be required in vast amounts if we are to follow where she led.

Notes

1. Leonard Bloomfield, *Language* (New York: Holt, 1933), p. 31.

2. Alexander L. Luria, *Cognitive Development: Its Cultural and Social Foundations*, trans. Martin Lopez-Morillas and Lynn Solotaroff (Cambridge: Harvard University Press, 1976), pp. v–vi.

3. Ibid., p. 13.

4. Ibid., p. 164.

Litəracy
part one

Law, Linguistics, and the English Language

Don't Grammar Count?

THOMAS H. MIDDLETON

Thomas Middleton loves words, and he loves to see them used with precision. He is the author of "Light Refractions," a column dealing largely with language in the Saturday Review, *and of "Double-Crostics," published by the* Saturday Review, *the* New York Times, *and Simon and Schuster.*

When Middleton is invited to speak to English teachers, he does not hestitate to chide them for subjecting their students to what he considers to be alarming trends in language and learning in the classroom. In this essay, he examines the teaching of English from the perspective of someone who earns a living as a writer.

I'm always flattered when I'm asked to address groups of professionals—writers, teachers, university professors, and in general people who get paid to deal with the English language. And I ask myself what I know that they don't know better—what they don't know more about. After all, they're experts, and I'm just a dilettante. Actually, to be truthful, I *used* to ask myself that question. Before I first spoke to the National Council of Teachers of English at their annual convention in New York a few years ago, I had the idea that all these teachers had pretty much the same goals that the English teachers of my youth had, and that that goal was to make their students more or less comfortable with what educated users of the language have thought of as its rules. At that time, I gave what I suppose was a pep talk, saying that it was obvious to me that a great many young people were looking for discipline, that they were hungry for rules and structure in their lives.

It wasn't long, of course, before I learned that a great many (though not, I think, most) of the teachers I was speaking to didn't agree with me that young people were looking for rules and that, furthermore, they had no intention of teaching what the teachers of my youth had taught. In fact, many of these teachers had decided, on the basis of some research or other, that the sort of education I had received in grade school was crippling to creativity, was in any case impossible for most youngsters to understand, had little if anything to recommend it, and was altogether a worthless program that did nothing but contribute to the undemocratic maintenance of an elitist ruling class. I learned that, for the past twenty years or more, hardly anyone had taught grammar rules. I also learned, to my extreme dismay, that those many teachers who continued to feel that rules were important and that they were not impossible to master had often been forbidden to teach them.

As I said, I learned this to my great dismay. I've seen some of the literature that purports to demonstrate that the teaching of grammar is detrimental and that it does nothing whatever to help people to think logically. The trouble with me is that every time I see the results of a study that tells me that something I've observed to be true for most of my life is actually false, I tend to question the study. I question my own observations, too, but mostly I question the study. After questioning my own observations about whether the study of grammar had any positive influence on my ability to think logically, I came once again to the unavoidable answer that grammar did, indeed, enhance my sense of logic. Then I questioned not only myself, but my friends and acquaintances to see if *they* thought that the study of grammar had helped them to think logically. All of them said it had, and, not surprisingly, many of them added that the study of mathematics—particularly algebra and geometry—had helped equally in this regard. Well, when all of us are convinced from our own experience that something has worked for us, it isn't easy to accept the dictates of someone who has performed some sort of experiment that proves we've been kidding ourselves. Call me narrow-minded, if you will, but I think there's a very good chance that my friends and I have a point.

I'm not a professional educator. I ask myself what I know better than professional English teachers. What can I tell them about, that I alone am a leading authority on? The answer is obvious: my mail. My mail, and the comments people make to me in casual conversation. Through no striving on my part, I seem to have stumbled quite by chance into a position that makes me a lodestar for thousands of people who care about the English language. I find it flattering, a bit frightening, and, above all, enlightening.

It shouldn't come as much of a surprise to you that much of my mail comes from people who lament the slipping standards of English usage, pronunciation, and grammar. As you might expect, most of this mail comes from people who are middle-aged and older, who learned "right" from "wrong" in their youth and who feel that hardly anyone cares any more. Television commentators, who should be setting good examples, speak of *nucular* energy and say things like, "It was a bad week for he and his family." "What," they ask, "is happening to our beautiful language?" This, of course, is understandable and predictable. We all tend to think that what we were taught when we were young is true and good and that any deviation from that truth and goodness is necessarily false and bad.

What might not be so predictable is that I also get a lot of mail from younger people who complain that they've never really learned any honest-to-God rules of the language. They want me to recommend books of grammar and usage. I'm very pleasantly surprised to find that young people are reading the *Saturday Review* when they could be watching *Starsky and Hutch* or *The Price is Right.*

This mail reaffirms my sense that an awful lot of people are looking for rules. In the final analysis, people simply can't function efficiently without rules—without limitations—without structure. In the past ten or fifteen years we've been going through a cataclysmic revolution in standards. What with the profound challenge to authority precipitated by Vietnam, the civil rights movement—black power—and the upheavals brought about by the modern feminist movement, there has, understandably, been a great cloud of doubt cast over almost all the values of the so-called Establishment. I can't think of anything that hasn't taken its knocks, from religion to the family to Kellogg's Sugar Pops.

All these revolutions have been justified, and some have been long overdue. But as with most revolutions, there have been some excesses and atrocities. We've gone through a time when many otherwise thoughtful people have said, in effect, that anything goes. Since so many of the old standards were unjust, then probably all of them were. Society is being shaken up, and the overriding principle has been "be yourself," whatever that means, and we find youngsters, even children, saying, "I gotta be me," and "I want to find out who I am."

We tell everyone that they can be anything and do anything, and that their options are unlimited. That sounds good, but most people really can't handle it, I think. Freedom, just as an abstract concept, is extremely difficult even to talk about intelligently. Most of us speak of freedom as though we knew exactly what it was. As though everyone knew what it is. But we don't. Just about everyone of my generation remembers a rhyme or two from the A. A. Milne books that were so popular during our childhood. There's one Milne rhyme the gist of which I've never forgotten. It's called *The Old Sailor,* and it poses one of the dilemmas of freedom. It begins:

> There was once an old sailor my grandfather knew
> Who had so many things which he wanted to do
> That whenever he thought it was time to begin
> He couldn't, because of the state he was in.

And it goes on to tell of how the old sailor was shipwrecked and lived on an island for weeks and he wanted a hat and he wanted some breeks, and so on, and every time he started working on the attainment of any of his desires, he'd think of another one. So, when he was trying to make a fish hook, he realized he needed a hat, and to make a hat, he'd need needle and thread, so he started to make a needle, then he immediately thought he'd better start building a boat. And so on. Anyway, the old sailor was in a situation in which he had no restraints, no channels, no orders to follow, no role to play. And so, in the end he did nothing at all but lie on the shingle, wrapped up in a shawl. And I think it was dreadful the way he behaved. He did nothing but basking until he was saved. It's a children's poem and a comical exaggeration, not to be taken very seriously, I suppose, but it does say something. Without discipline, without structure, most of us flounder and do nothing.

I was sitting in a park a couple of weeks ago, working on a column for the *Saturday Review*. I was at one of those picnic tables, engrossed in my writing, when two young mothers came over and sat down across the table from me, with their backs to me. Their children were playing on the slides nearby, and one of the women was saying, "Michael needs structure. He was in an open-structured class, and he was a problem. Then they put him in a more structured class, and there's a tremendous difference."

I apologized for intruding, and, getting off the obligatory cliché about how I couldn't help overhearing, I asked her if she'd tell me more about Michael. She said that Michael, at age seven, had been floundering about, accomplishing nothing in an open-structured school which he hated. Then they moved him into a more structured class, and he came home absolutely ecstatic, because he had *his own desk! His own place.* And she said that Michael was functioning much better now that he had been put into a sort of slot of his own. He had been given a structure within which to work. She added that her other three children had all had the same experience.

It was this woman's telling me about Michael, age seven, that made me think of the old sailor in that children's poem, which, incidentally, comes from a book called *Now We Are Six.* If there's a moral here, it might be that unlimited freedom is no freedom at all. Self-discipline is the ideal discipline, of course, but I think only one person in a thousand is innately so inner-directed that he can *create* his own self-discipline and invent his own structure. We need, all of us, at least in our early years, to have rules: rules of behavior, and—let's face it—rules of the language laid on us from above, from figures of authority.

I don't know who first said it, but one of my favorite statements—not really a statement, but a rhetorical question—is, How do I know what I think until I've put it in writing? Writing is, indeed, the test of thinking. Only when one has written one's thoughts can one marshall them, criticize them, change them in a constructive way, and, of course, communicate them effectively to other human beings. And clear writing depends upon the understanding of certain rules. There has been a tendency recently to say that the rules of the language, like the rules of so many of our other traditions, are irrelevant. Well, they are not. They are very relevant. Good writers frequently break the rules. But good writers *know* the rules, and they know when and why they are breaking them.

I'm sure you're all thoroughly familiar with Fowler's *Modern English Usage,* and with his masterful discussion of the split infinitive. The section on the split infinitive is a fairly long but very brilliant piece of writing which I'll not go into in detail. His first paragraph, you may remember, says, "The English-speaking world may be divided into (one) those who neither know nor care what a split infinitive is; (two) those who do not know but care very much; (three) those who know and condemn; (four) those who know and approve; and (five) those who know and distinguish."

I think this principle might be extrapolated to cover the relationship of the English-speaking world with the rules of grammar in general. One: there are those who neither know nor care. Two: there are those who do not know but care very much. This category is of special interest to me, because I get a surprising amount of mail from people who complain bitterly about bits of usage which they believe to be abominations in the sight of the Lord, but which are, in fact, perfectly acceptable idioms that could have been validated by simply consulting a good dictionary. Three: those who know and condemn. They're the purists. The ones who parse sentences for the sheer joy of it. They know their stuff, and they condemn solecisms at every opportunity. They want to outlaw not only split infinitives, but prepositions at the end of sentences, and if you say, "Try and stop me," they'll come down hard, correcting it to "Try *to* stop me."

The fourth category: those who know and approve. Of course, in Fowler's discussion, they simply approve of the use of split infinitives. Fowler says that evidently they do so "as a manifesto of independence." To my mind, this fourth category is a deplorable one. These are the educated people who know the rules, but have made the conscious decision that the rules are not only not important but are evidence of this terrible crime known as *elitism.* They break the rules because they've decided the rules exist only to serve some sort of counterrevolutionary function. The fifth category—the band of angels— are those who know and distinguish. These are the best writers, those who know the rules and know when and why they are breaking them.

Today, we're cursed with some very special problems. From what I've heard and read, we have on the one hand a vast army of young people who have been awarded high school diplomas, but have somehow avoided learning to write. I hear that they haven't simply avoided learning to write *well;* they've avoided learning to write at all. Diplomas notwithstanding, they are uneducated.

On the other hand, we have the supereducated, the men and women with doctoral degrees, who cannot, or will not, write simple declarative sentences. These are the ones who, for any number of reasons, insist on using awkward words in an obscurant style so that no one can readily understand what they're talking about. If I may quote good old Fowler again, this time on *officialese:*

> It is a style of writing marked by peculiarities supposed to be characteristic of officials. If a single word were needed to describe those peculiarities, that chosen by Dickens—circumlocution—is still the most suitable. They may be ascribed to a combination of causes: a feeling that plain words assort ill with the dignity of office; a politeness that shrinks from blunt statements; and, above all, the knowledge that for those engaged in the perilous game of politics, and their servants, vagueness is safer than precision.
>
> The natural result is stilted and verbose style, not readily intelligible, a habit of mind, for instance, that automatically rejects the adjective *unsightly* in favor of the periphrasis *detrimental to the visual amenities of the locality.*

Fowler also has a piece on *sociologese.* We're all familiar with that style. The fact is that just about every discipline in the world today seems to have developed its own -*ese.* To me, the most depressing of all the -*eses* is *educationese.* Educators, of all people, should make sense to as many people as possible. But I've received in my mail many examples of the most preposterous gobbledegook written by educators.

I won't depress you by inflicting many samples on you, but I have chosen one that was sent to me by a woman who wrote:

> Dear Mr. Middleton,
>
> I thought you would be interested in the enclosed letter sent by the chairman of the English department of a New York state high school. Can you imagine this man teaching the "advantaged student"? (Every chairman I've ever known taught only honor students.)

Later she says:

You call it educationese; we call it garbage.

Here's the letter. I've crossed off the name of the man who wrote it. I don't want to embarrass him, though I'd like to shake him up a bit. He is, indeed—or at least he was—the chairman of the English department of a high school in New York State. The letter says:

> Dear Dr. Nyquist:
>
> Salutations.

(Evidently, this guy doesn't know that "Dear Dr. Nyquist" is what is called a salutation.) Anyway, he says:

> Dear Dr. Nyquist:
>
> Salutations. Since my original letter to you of July 5, 1974 in which I clarified the role of NYSEC in exploring and defining Performance Based Teacher Certification, the communicative dialog from State Education department personnel entrusted by you to work in conjunction with NYSEC has unfortunately slowed the anticipatory progress expected of educational colleagues. The attenuation of this interchange demeans the role of those delegated by you to seek harmoniously the pertinent goals to achieve a satisfactory blend of understanding *now* must be noted. This impingement has caused the CETTS chairman to redefine his position relative to the State's original response in effecting an open communicative avenue of commitment.

I won't bore you with the whole letter, but the last paragraph is really a pip:

> Therefore, at this time, I lay before you the problematical realization that those who expedite the State's mandate border on the arrogation of this responsibility tending to disrupt and discredit the very principle of educational leadership explicit in your earlier directive as the Commissioner of Education. The expectation of rekindling the democratic flame rests with you.

The lady who sent this closes by saying:

Down with educationese! Away with garbage! Say it simply!

I think that, if I were a teacher of English, I'd have two plaques made that I'd carry with me to every single class or seminar. One would say, "Say it simply" and the other would say, "How do I know what I think until I've put it in writing?"

It is my feeling that anyone who writes in a style even remotely resembling that of our anonymous chairman of the English department should do himself a favor and take a dollar and a half and buy The Little Book: William Strunk and E. B. White's *The Elements of Style*. He should then copy out every word of it in longhand. It wouldn't be too arduous a task. It really is quite a *little* book. But it would be worth every minute and every twinge of writer's cramp. He should then read Fowler's *Modern English Usage* from cover to cover.

Young people are suffering from not having been taught the rules of the language. I am certain of that. It isn't just my mail that tells me; it's the unprecedented catastrophe in America's colleges, where entering freshmen don't know the meaning of subject and predicate, adverb, adjective, and preposition. It is common for the antigrammarian teachers to point out that complaints about the illiteracy of the younger generation have been common for centuries and, indeed, for millennia. But on examination, it appears that those complaints historically have usually been based on perceptions of form and meaning—the normal reluctance of an older generation to admit that words and forms have undergone a natural alteration in the course of time. Today, many thousands of high school graduates are incapable of writing understandable sentences. It is no longer a matter of oldfogeyish nit-picking about whether *contact* is or is not a verb or some such nicety of usage. The problem now, since the cessation of training in the traditional rules of language, has become one of simple intelligibility.

In his excellent book, *Less Than Words Can Say* (Boston: Little, Brown, 1979), Richard Mitchell cites several examples of unintelligible writing by college students and, indeed, by college teachers. Let me read only one, a relatively short one. This is an application for a schoolteaching job. Mitchell quotes from four such applications, all written not by college freshmen but by college graduates. I choose this one simply because it is the shortest of the four. It is no worse than the other three:

> In the process of teaching science to students there will be preassessment test to determine what the student already knows. From the finding of the preassessment test objectives, teacher and students will be designed. Concepts to be taught will be listed. If the subject area being covered is weather, then the different aspects of weather will be introduced. There will be worksheets and experiment to prove and evaluate the objectives for the activity. The activity children will be given activities that they will have to do on their own example collecting date of the formation of clouds and what weather usually follow certain cloud formation. The project must be flexable so that it meets the need of each child and is meaningful for them.

On April 2, 1978, the *New York Times* (sec. 4, p. 19) carried an article by a young woman named Edna Goldsmith, a literate woman—in fact, a graduate in literature from Yale University. Ms. Goldsmith said that even after having gone through Yale, she didn't know much about where to place commas:

> When I finally thought of consulting a grammar handbook, I was shocked to discover that just to begin to understand commas I had to go through the entire book. My B.A. notwithstanding, I

was a girl who barely knew what a clause was. While I'm not proud of this, in my defense it must be said that I was also a girl who barely had been taught what a clause was.

In elementary school the "language arts" teacher came to my class once or twice a week and ate pretzels. She intrigued me, but she did not teach me how to diagram a sentence. Neither did anyone in my junior high school, because my junior high school was "progressive" and did not "believe" in grammar. And if my high school believed in grammar, the teachers still did not believe in teaching it. A little grammar here, a little grammar there, that's all I got in high school.

There is no doubt in my mind that I should have gotten more. Not only more instruction in the fundamentals of grammar, but also more instruction in the elements of composition. While my ignorance in matters grammatical did not seriously damage my academic performance in college—even without "knowing" grammar, I had never been one to dangle modifiers—it did mean that I had to spend time learning basics that I should have been taught earlier.

Now that I have studied these basics, I write more clearly and more logically; also, now that commas no longer mystify me, I write more quickly.

Ms. Goldsmith echoes precisely those points that come to me in my mailbox weekly.

The most distressing pieces of mail I get are from people who either teach English or are intending to teach English, but whose qualifications are evidently inadequate. Several years ago, I got a long treatise written by a university professor and a graduate student in English. I recall that it seemed an unusual collaboration, since the professor taught at a state university in the Midwest and the grad student attended a state university in an adjacent state. The professor was a woman and the student was a man. All of this is quite beside the point, but it was by far the most interesting aspect of the paper, which was on *nominalization:* the making of nouns from other word forms and the overuse of nouns in preference to other words. The paper was loaded with percentages and other statistics and was quite dull, but this was back when I was younger and kinder, and so, because I was kind, or chicken, or polite, or too busy, or a combination of these, I simply thanked the authors for their very interesting paper. What I found particularly distressing, though, was the misspellings. I know it isn't considered chic these days to carp about misspellings, but I do think that professors of English and graduate students in English should be held accountable for these niceties. The authors maintained, perhaps correctly, that the modern overuse of nouns resulted from an attempt to impart a magisterial tone to the writing. But in every case, they spelled magisterial *majesterial.* Of course, that's the kind of thing that's hard to look up. If you think magisterial begins *m-a-j,* you look it up under *maj,* and you're likely to conclude either that there's no such word or that you're using a lousy dictionary. In any case, it did disturb me that a professor of English and, presumably, a future professor of English would stay with that misspelling. Even more disturbing, though, was their constant use of *logicly* and *publically.* Those two are easy to look up.

Another paper came to me, written by a woman who is either a teacher or a graduate student, on the subject of teaching children how to punctuate. She maintains that just teaching children the rules of punctuation and then testing them on what they have been taught is not nearly as good a method as letting children write and having them ask the teacher when they should punctuate and with what punctuation mark.

I couldn't possibly disagree with her; but she has completely ignored what seems to be to be the sensible alternative to either method: teach the children the rules of punctuation, have them write their own papers, and let them know what they've done right and what they've done wrong, and tell them why what is wrong is wrong. (Incidentally, Fowler, again, is my absolute favorite on punctuation. Any teacher who hasn't read Fowler's section under *stops* will do himself and his students a great favor by doing so. It's clear and refreshing. Enjoyable reading, if you care about such things.)

The depressing thing about this young woman's paper (I'm assuming she's young on the basis of her lack of knowledge of what she's talking about) is that she doesn't seem to know the first thing about the rules of punctuation. She seems, in fact, totally unaware that there *are* such things as rules for the placement of commas. We all know that there are innumerable situations in which the use of a comma is discretionary, and we all know that sometimes the hard-and-fast rules for the comma can be broken. But if we are unaware that there are—no kidding—specific instances in which commas are called for and other instances in which commas can be disastrous, then we have no right preparing papers on how to teach children punctuation. One interesting aspect of this paper (interesting to me, at any rate) is that the author thinks a caret is a punctuation mark. She makes this quite clear, and actually speaks of teaching the proper use of the caret, which she constantly spells *carot*. A caret, as we all know, is a sign that we have forgotten something and would like to put it in. It is a simple obvious reminder of human fallibility. It has nothing to do with punctuation, and anyone who cannot master its use in less than a minute must have serious learning problems.

Evidently, the woman who wrote this paper on punctuation had approximately the same sort of education as Edna Goldsmith had. The difference between the two is that, after graduating from Yale, Ms. Goldsmith decided to learn about punctuation, whereas the other woman will probably con some school board into paying her for teaching children what she herself never learned.

Not surprisingly, I get lots of mail from parents who are infuriated about teachers who don't know their subject. Here's one I got recently. It's typical of literally hundreds I've received over the years:

Dear Mr. Middleton:

Your column is right on target. It reminds me of one time some years ago when I confronted an "English teacher" at the then prestigious Evanston, Illinois, Township High School. This gent had marked my son's paper wrong where he'd written "different from" and had crossed out that phrase and written in its place "different *than*." My seasoned editorial hackles rose and I went to investigate the cretin. He asked me to name my authority for the correct usage, and when I cited *Webster's International*, he said, pityingly, "You really mean you use the *dictionary* as an authority?" "Yes," I said, "and what do you use?" The inevitable reply came back quickly: "Why, *usage*, of course."

This teacher evidently saw nothing wrong with using his own personal perceptions of "usage" in marking the paper. That's one of the problems with this wonderful criterion of "usage." Whose usage? Mine? Jimmy Breslin's? Mickey Mantle's? Usage, of course, alters the language. Language is in a state of flux, because it lives. Nevertheless, we bend to every caprice of change at our peril. Clear communication depends upon some documented rules of meaning and of expression, on maintaining a continuity.

When I speak of rules and discipline, I realize I'm putting myself in a vulnerable spot. I'll be called reactionary, hidebound, Neanderthal, Prussian, and a slew of less complimentary terms. I am not a Prussian, however. I have no objection to colloquialisms. I think colorful, expressive language is just that: colorful and expressive.

And I love it. The crux of my thesis is that English is one of the world's great languages. Probably more people on every continent are making an effort to learn English than any other language. And the English they want to learn is something referred to rather vaguely as "standard English." It is not the "language that students have their right to." Everyone certainly has a right to speak any language he likes, from classic Latin to Cockney rhyming slang and pig Latin. But I think that every child in the United States has the right to be instructed in approximately the same English that is being taught all over the world. And I think they should be told that this is the English that is accepted by—what? By educated people? By the folks with the power? By elitists? By the dictionaries? The books on modern English usage? It doesn't matter which you choose. The fact is that it is an important language with an important and fascinating history. English has been influenced by countless other tongues and dialects. Like any other skill, or art form, or whatever term you choose, the language can best be understood, I think, by those who are given a grounding in its classic system. To argue that that system is arbitrary is to miss an important point. The system is a useful tool not only in mastering English, but in discerning its relationship to other languages of the Western world.

To argue the relative merits or truth or reality of the written word versus the spoken word is a fascinating and valuable exercise, but it also misses the point. The record of the language is in its writing; and, as I've said before and will doubtless say again, writing is an essential tool for the reasoning process. How do I know what I think until I've put it in writing?

Those writers who best express the product of their reasoning are those who have mastered the structure of the language. A few—a very few—geniuses have been able to work wonders with the language without having studied its structure. But to have learned the structure, whether the structure is arbitrary or not (and that itself is a moot point) is to have a priceless grounding in a priceless skill.

Los Angeles, California

Literacy: A Human and a Legal Problem

VIVIAN I. DAVIS

*Vivian Davis has been a member of the Executive
Committee of the National Council of Teachers of
English and chairwoman of the Conference on College
Composition and Communication. She received her
A.B. from Ball State Teachers College, her M.A.T. from
the University of Chicago, and her Ph.D. from
Northwestern University. She has recently studied
public school law at Texas Woman's University, from
which she received the M.Ed.*

*Davis began her teaching career as a Spanish
instructor at Prairie View A&M College in Texas. In
this essay she addresses both legal and human
problems that minority students face in an educational
system that is often insensitive or uninformed.*

Today education is perhaps the most important function of state
and local governments. Compulsory school attendance laws and
the great expenditures for education both demonstrate our recognition of the importance of education to our democratic society. It is required in the performance of our most basic public
responsibilities, even service in the armed forces. It is the very
foundation of good citizenship. Today it is a principal instrument
in awakening the child to cultural values, in preparing him for
later professional training and in helping him to adjust normally to his environment. In these days, it is doubtful that any
child may reasonably be expected to succeed in life if he is denied
the opportunity of an education. Such an opportunity, where the

state has undertaken to provide it, is a right which must be
made available to all on equal terms.[1]

That statement was the cornerstone of the landmark
case, *Brown* v. *Board of Education of Topeka, Kansas,*
1954. Mr. Justice Warren, writing the majority opinion of
the Supreme Court, not only set the precedence for deseg-
regation of American public schools, but ushered in a
new era in American education. For the first time, the
highest court in the land defined education as a right to
be made equally available to all. Based on this premise
that education is an implicit right of citizenship, other
plaintiffs since 1954 have petitioned courts not only to
desegregate schools, but to demolish whatever barriers
hinder citizens from equal access to educational opportunity. While those barriers have been both physical and
mental, more directly related to our deliberations here
are those specifically defined as language barriers. From
a legal point of view these are the most problematic
barriers of all. Physical handicaps and severe mental
handicaps are relatively easy to identify; distinguishing
between a language handicap and language difference is
a much more elusive and politically explosive matter. Yet
lawmakers and judges have had to assume the responsibility for establishing policies about language when
English teachers themselves seem unable to agree on
what those policies should be.

When the barrier has been a second language (rather
than a second dialect), the courts have been consistent in
requiring that schools provide appropriate language instruction for non-English-speaking students in the public schools. In the case of *Lau* v. *Nichols,* 1974, the United
States Supreme Court observed that children who speak
a language other than English and who are not instructed in the use of English are, as far as school is

concerned, without any language at all.[2] These children, the Court found, experienced a language barrier which denies them their opportunity of equal access to education. Consequently, their Fourteenth Amendment rights are violated. The Court ordered San Francisco public schools to provide appropriate language instruction for Chinese-American children who needed to learn English in order to profit from education. San Francisco protested it did not have the money; the Court demanded compliance. A similar case in New Mexico forced the schools there to make the same provision for Spanish-speaking children.

But even when the courts order barriers to be removed, the system seems to be in no hurry to comply. Bilingual education in Texas, for example, has been brought to a standstill by a recently appointed commissioner of education who decided that there should be no increase in bilingual education until the effect of present programs in the state has been researched. Of course he proposed no way to study or evaluate what is presently being done. Perhaps there is no need to: without the benefit of a study, my Chicano friends can tell him that far too many children who could possibly profit from a bilingual program have never had the opportunity to be involved in one.

And the spirit of compliance is often ungenerous, sometimes downright mean. Even before the courts had had a chance to decide whether Dallas Independent School District must provide education to illegal aliens, one principal, zealous in what he believed was his duty to rout undeserving children from the classroom, dismissed two Spanish-speaking sisters, one in the talented and gifted program at his elementary school, but both native-born Americans. He thought the children spoke only

Spanish and lived with grandparents, which made him
suspect that they were attending school illegally.

The problem becomes even stickier when separate dialects are involved, since the public—even the educated
public—finds it difficult to grant minority dialects the
same status it gives to foreign languages. Dialectal differences became a legal issue in Florida when, in the
mid-seventies, the legislature directed the Department
of Education of the state to develop a statewide program
for the assessment of student achievement in basic skills.
The legislature also established three requirements for
high school graduation: completion of regular academic
course work, mastery of basic skills, and functional literacy. In the spring and fall of 1978 and spring of 1979
minimal competency tests for math and language skills
were given to juniors and seniors in the Florida public
schools. There was a marked difference in the pass-fail
rates of whites and blacks. Even after a year of remedial
work, blacks failed the tests ten times as often as whites.

The case was taken to court as *Debra P. v. Turlington*.[3]
The plaintiffs argued that the tests were culturally
biased; the program was discriminatory in that it assigned black students who failed to remedial classes and
denied them high school diplomas. They argued further
that these black students, as victims of a segregated
system, had not received equal or adequate education;
and that even after integration, they had been victims of
unequal disciplinary punishment, hostility, and the loss
of black teachers and counselors in the schools. Furthermore, the plaintiffs argued, there had not been time
enough for these students to prepare for the tests before
they were required to pass them or lose their right to a
high school diploma.

On July 12, 1979, the United States District Court for
the Middle District of Florida ruled that the tests could

be used as diagnostic instruments to identify students who needed help in learning academic skills. The judge stipulated that this use of the tests was allowable even though it would result in part-time remedial programs in most Florida districts where there were concentrations of blacks and segregated schools, *only* because there was no evidence that the remedial courses could not realistically compensate students whose failure of the tests resulted from past segregation. Following the advice of expert witnesses, that there should be a minimum of four to six years between the announcement and the implementation of the testing program to allow blacks time to be prepared, the judge ruled that quick implementation of the testing program would violate the Fourteenth Amendment rights of the students. He ruled that making the passing of the tests a requirement for graduation be held off for four years. This ruling, according to the judge, was the least possible interference with the state's duty to protect the constitutional rights of the students.

On the same date in July 1979 Judge Charles W. Joiner of the U.S. District Court, Eastern District of Michigan, Southern Division, handed down a decision in a case that dealt even more directly with barriers related to dialectal differences in a school where there had been no history of segregation. The case, *Martin Luther King, Junior, Elementary School Children et al. v. Ann Arbor School District Board*,[4] had been initiated in July 1977 by fifteen black preschool and elementary school children who claimed that the board and certain individual teachers and administrators had violated their rights by determining that they were all eligible for special education based on learning difficulties. The plaintiffs alleged that the defendants had not determined whether their learning difficulty stemmed from cultural, social, or economic deprivation. They demanded to know the bases of the children's deprivation and to have a program established that would enable them to overcome their deprivation so that they could progress normally in school.

In deliberating the case, the judge found no evidence that Ann Arbor currently operates or has ever operated a dual school system. The school in question is located in a liberal, middle-class neighborhood and has a population approximately 80 percent white, 13 percent black, and 7 percent Asian or other. The sole remaining issue, finally, was whether the children's rights as protected by Title 20 of the U.S. code were denied them because the children's use of black English as their home language constituted a barrier to their acquisition of standard English, the language of the school.

Judge Joiner set himself the task of determining whether the children's use of black English as their home language was in fact a barrier to their learning the language of the school and thereby a barrier to their access to equal educational opportunity. The judge heard the expert testimony of linguists regarding the definition of black English and what effect it could have on the children's learning standard English, as well as what remedies were reasonable. The judge also questioned school officials and teachers to determine the nature of the curriculum and the materials and teaching approaches used with the children. He found that the school provided counselors, tutors, speech therapists, and other specialists to work with the students. He found also that the school used some of the same materials and approaches recommended by the linguists.

The judge also found, on the other hand, that neither the school nor the individual teachers recognized black English as a language with the status of the home languages that children of other ethnic backgrounds bring to the school. Some teachers did, however, recognize and speak black English from time to time in their work with the children. No attempt was made on the part of the teachers to humiliate children who used black English.

Judge Joiner also questioned the children who were plaintiffs in the suit. He found them "attractive, likeable, at times shy, youngsters." Their speech, though it contained traces of black English, was intelligible, and they understood standard English. They appeared able to adapt quickly to standard English "in settings where it appears to be the proper language."

The judge found the school and the teachers did attempt to help the children. Nonetheless, he also found that the black dialect or vernacular used at home by black students in general makes it more difficult for such children to learn to read for three reasons:

1. the lack of parental or other home support in the provision of models who read, enjoy, and profit from skills in standard English;
2. the students' experience of difficulty in hearing and making certain sounds used in standard English but not distinguished in their home language;
3. the psychological barrier to student learning caused by the unconscious but evident attitude of teachers toward the home language.

Futher, Judge Joiner found that one cause of the children's failure to learn to read could be the failure of the Ann Arbor School District to develop a program to assist teachers to take account of the children's home language in teaching standard English; and that it is the school system's obligation to take appropriate action to overcome the language barrier. The judge warned that school officials must not act blindly, callously, or thoughtlessly, but "must have as their goal the Congressional requirement, the elimination of existing language barriers, and the steps that they take must be rational and logical in light of the situation confronting them and the knowledge reasonably available to them."

The defendant school board was ordered to submit to the court within thirty days a proposed plan defining the exact steps to be taken to help the teachers identify black English-speaking students and to use that knowledge in teaching standard English to those children. According to newspaper accounts, the Ann Arbor School Board did submit a proposal to the judge, but it was defective in that it included the use of a diagnostic test that could not distinguish whether the children's errors were a function of their lack of knowledge or ability or a function of their use of black English. At least that part of the plan was not acceptable to the court.

I have gone into much detail to spell out some landmark cases that I think illustrate some of the reasons why literacy, at least in America, is a very human problem. I do not wish to trace here the long, tortuous history which would more clearly illustrate the problem black Americans have had in acquiring literacy. Suffice it to say that the question of whether or not blacks had the right to literacy at all has been a controversial one laden with complex ambiguities. Part of the time blacks were not to be allowed to learn to read and write because it would so humanize them as to make then unfit for slavery. At other times blacks were not to become literate because, since they reportedly lacked the capacity to learn anyway, there was no sense in wasting the effort and mistreating them by requiring something of them they could not possibly do; their attempting it would only frustrate them. On the other hand, blacks have rarely had the opportunity to speak for themselves in matters concerning their right to literacy and more broadly to education. To be sure, they have had the responsibility of being taxed for the support of literacy for other groups in the society, and sometimes they have physically built the buildings that housed the classes in which whites learned how to read and write. But the power relationships in American society have successfully made the question of literacy for blacks in particular, but also for other unempowered groups, a tenuous privilege they have had to beg of the society.

Let's note again what happened in the courts and what the effect of that has been for the unempowered. I hardly need to recall the generation's delay that the Supreme Court itself made possible in its doctrine of "all deliberate speed." In the meantime those states that most flagrantly abused the black citizens' right to equal access to educational opportunity continued to do so. A very revealing study conducted among adult illiterates by Theodore James Pinnock of the Tuskegee Institute points out the many barriers to black literacy imposed up to this very decade, perhaps right at this very moment. The study (written, incidentally, without the use of the apostrophe designating possession) points out the most subtle roadblocks that prevented rural poor blacks from attaining even the most rudimentary education.[5] I shall not review the study here, trusting you to read it. I do want to mention just one blatant barrier, since busing has been such a big controversy in our recent attempts to make equal educational opportunity for all a reality. Black schools were as likely as not to be located as far as ten miles away from the students' homes in rural communities. No transportation was provided. Children were expected to walk as far as twenty miles daily to attend school. What time must they have had to leave home in the mornings? And when should they expect to return in the evenings? Small wonder more female than male students were reported dropping out before they completed elementary school.

Not only did the 1954 decision allow for delay in providing equal opportunity, but the courts themselves have acted very slowly even when they have acted favorably. In the case of *Martin Luther King, Junior, Elementary School* v. *Ann Arbor School District Board* it took two years for the court to rule in favor of the plaintiffs. Only eleven of the fifteen original plaintiffs remained in the suit by the time a ruling was handed down. Furthermore, Judge Joiner refused to allow the case class action status, and, had the Ann Arbor School District Board chosen to do so, it might have appealed the case to the district court and even to the Supreme Court, should that court have agreed to hear it.

We have to note too the very strict view the courts have taken in intervening in school matters. It is in fact the unwritten rule of the courts that local schools be interfered with as little as possible. That rule kept the Supreme Court from mandating a change in the taxing system in Texas in the 1974 case of *San Antonio Independent School District* v. *Rodriguez*.[6] Mr. Rodriguez sued because students in Rosedale, an impoverished section of San Antonio, were not getting equal education opportunity when compared with the educational opportunity afforded their more affluent neighbors. The court found that unequal taxation in the state did affect the quality of education that poorer children could get. Nonetheless, it found that poor children were not being denied their rights, because the state of Texas was providing a fundamental educational program for all children. The court also advised that the matter of finding an equitable taxing system rested properly with the legislators of the state of Texas. As you may guess, little has been done to equalize the educational opportunity of poor children in Texas.

The courts have, in common parlance, opened a can of worms. The instinctive reaction of many people concerned about education is to turn back the clock and expect the worms to crawl back into the can. The past, however, did not really solve the problems we are aware of today; it simply avoided them. In their historical exploration of the nature of literacy, Daniel and Lauren Resnick point out that our society demands a mass literacy that is more widely applied than any standard of literacy we have ever had. They say:

> Unless we intend to relinquish the criterion of comprehension as the goal of reading instruction, there is little to go *back* to in terms of pedagogical method, curriculum, or school organization. The old tried and true approaches, which nostalgia prompts us to believe might solve current problems, were designed neither to achieve the literacy standard sought today nor to assure successful literacy for everyone. Whatever the rhetoric of the common school, early dropping out and selective promotion were in fact used to escape problems that must now be addressed through a pedagogy adequate to today's aspirations. While we may be able to borrow important ideas and practices from earlier periods, there is no simple past to which we can return.[7]

As the Resnicks point out, the demand for universal literacy is not only itself a new demand, but there is little or nothing from the past academic repertoire to meet the challenge. Dropping out of school is not as common now as it was in the early sixties, and the courts are reluctant to allow school systems to warehouse unsuccessful students in remedial courses or in lower tracks. At the heart of it, the courts are asking on behalf of the unempowered that we teach them, that if there are barriers we remove them, so everyone will have equal access to educational opportunity. I would rather side with the courts. If there are barriers to making education accessible to all equally, we should be about the business of getting rid of them. That is both a more interesting and more creative place to start.

I believe, however, that academicians, teachers, are terrified at this mandate. I think we find it more comforting and certainly less risky to deliberate about the definition of literacy, or dialects, or grapholects, or students' right to their own language or even simplistic notions, like John Simon's that we need only to indoctrinate the kids with what they and we both know is right and good for them—our own brands of standard, eloquent, correct English. I have said before, we do not know what we are doing, and now I must add that I fear we are using deliberations about literacy as an escape. To loosely paraphrase Leon Botstein's statement about liberal arts in the universities today, literacy is now being too often used as a slogan to shield more serious social, cultural, and, I will add, economic and political issues from being addressed.[8] We as English teachers have operated out of social myths as much as any other human beings, often defending them without confronting them. Too often we have believed that we were acting for the students' highest good. Now I think we, as a profession, will have to get down to serious business and begin to grapple with how to solve the very human problem of teaching more kids and more adults how to read and write, preferably to free them from the illusion that power and prestige rightly belong to those who have acquired or inherited fluency in superficial language codes. That, in our profession, as least as I see it, is the new frontier.

There is much more that we have to learn than we know about how to teach literacy skills. I want to point out just a few areas that merit our concern. We know very little about language acquisition beyond infancy and early childhood, yet illiteracy cannot be identified as a problem except for adolescents and adults. We know nothing substantial about the development of the interior language that cognitive psychologists tell us is necessary to conceptualize, to create, to control one's own behavior. We know less about how interior language functions to allow the person to externalize thoughts in spoken or written form. I remember thinking when I studied Chomskian grammar that it might be much more useful to look for the strategies one used in deep structure than to worry so much about how transformations operate to produce surface structure.

I think if we would improve our teaching of literacy skills, especially writing, we will have to begin to approach writing as problem solving. We have to learn, and we have to teach our students, the heuristics that give one control over the writing process. I think we have to demystify writing and help our students to become conscious of what it is that keeps them from being able to render their thoughts and experiences successfully in writing. To be able to do this, we need to take more care to analyze the skills students need to perform the writing tasks we ask them to do. After such analyses, we need to build the kind of curricula by which students can learn the skills they need in the sequence in which they need them. And we need to provide our students ample opportunity to develop those skills. I should make it clear that when I speak of skills I am not talking about such things as building paragraphs, or writing complete sentences, or even knowing how to write descriptions or arguments. I am referring to the kinds of skills one needs to be able to guide a reader through a description or an argument; to imagine the other side in order to make an argument persuasive or at least rational. These skills are not dependent upon dialect, but they are fundamental to the writing process. However, most students are never brought to consciousness about the need to develop and to use such skills in their expositions.

English teachers are certainly not entirely to blame if they do not know what in the world to do with a class of partly literate adults. Most of us have not been taught how to teach anyone to write. I would propose that the person who aspires to teaching language skills needs first to learn those skills well enough to be fluent and highly proficient—the English teacher does have to know how to read and write. Every language skills teacher from kindergarten through university needs a good grounding in linguistics. I do not mean by that a course in the history of the English language, though I have nothing against people knowing that history. One ought to be able to define language and dialect and to distinguish between language as a generic phenomenon and the English language. The literacy teacher ought to understand the universalities that are common to all language and the variations that make one language different from other languages. Teachers should know that language is bound to the context out of which it develops, and they should know something of the psychological and sociological aspects of acquiring and using language. English teachers ought to understand more than one dialect of English. Of course they do, though they may not be conscious of it. Given all this knowledge, one has to have a healthy respect for the human mind and for human beings.

I cannot help but mention Mina Shaughnessy's *Errors and Expectations*.[9] What strikes me about the book is Shaughnessy's attempt to get into the minds of her students in order to understand enough about the ways they perceive what they are doing to be able to gently guide them, or not so gently to prod them toward more conscious control over their work. She uses the errors analysis approach to the teaching of writing, but she locates the sources of her students' miscues not in themselves, but in their inexperience with the print code, in mislearnings and partial learnings about standard English usage and grammar, in dialect interference, and in psychologically explainable habits. By recognizing that partly literate students do have the capacity to think and the ability to increase their skills in writing, Shaughnessy accepts the humanity of her students and thereby liberates herself to teach them.

I do not want to leave you thinking that Mina Shaughnessy was a great teacher because she loved and respected her students and understood that they were human beings. She did do that, and as I have said, that liberated her to *teach* them. There are too many white missionaries in black classrooms, and they are not all Caucasians. There is nothing especially wrong with being either white or a missionary, but one needs to be constantly aware that the ultimate goal, preferably while the student is in your class, is to enable the student to acquire or sharpen or further develop some literacy skills. It is that, rather than to show the kids how liberal or empathetic you are.

I have never been able to understand how English teachers could read the "Students' Right to Their Own Language" and come away with the notion that it is a mandate to abandon their role of teaching language skills in the classroom. Of course I know that the document clearly stipulates what the courts are now mandating, that teachers have to find out a great deal more than they know; that they will have to admit that their own attitudes, though never spoken, impart to their students a sense of superiority over anyone who does not hew to the teachers' brand of English. I am reminded, when I think of the fit so many teachers pitched after the students' manifesto, of an incident Richard Wright relates in *Black Boy*. You may remember it. He brought his cat into the house one day while his father, who worked at night, was trying to sleep. The cat was whining. Wright's father, sleepless, demanded that Richard quiet the cat. The boy wanted to know how he could keep the cat still, and the old man, without thinking, growled, "Kill him." Richard, not being particularly fond of his father anyhow, saw that as his opportunity to get even with the old man. He took the cat out and killed it.

One wonders how many English teachers are killing the cat when they claim that if they have to take account of the students' dialects, they cannot teach them how to write, or speak, or read, or anything else. Respecting the students' rights does not absolve teachers from their responsibility to teach; it simply requires them to teach with an informed and healthy appreciation of the language the student brings to the classroom. There is a great deal more I would say about teacher preparation and teacher effectiveness if this were a different occasion. The competence of teachers, for example, is every bit as sticky an issue as the competence of students. I once heard on the radio the tail end of some newscaster's report on the latest poll (Gallup Poll, I presume) indicating that a majority of Americans believe that teachers should pass some kind of qualifying exam, perhaps like the bar or medical exam (I thought about the beauty culturalist exam), in order to be licensed, and that teachers should have to submit periodically to tests that would determine whether they were keeping current in their disciplines. It was of no little interest to me that the public seems to want more from its teachers than it wants from its doctors or lawyers.

I, too, believe we need and in fact will have to develop (before someone does it for us) useful ways of determining that teachers are adequately prepared for the language classroom. And I believe that as a profession we will have to do more about the quality of teacher training than making pronouncements such as I have done here. I am not sure how we can go about it. I know the Conference on College Composition and Communication abandoned the notion of becoming an accrediting agency.

Let me simply end by saying that the future in literacy is an open field. I think the court decisions I mentioned here will have a great impact on the direction we will take in the near future, but there will be more beyond that, which will demand the best of us. I do not believe English teachers are naturally backward. I think we can be equal to the task.

I do want to issue a caveat or two. Right now the courts are in a mood to call us back to our responsibility of removing the barriers to opportunity, including language barriers. Black people, especially, know a great deal about the moods of the courts; consequently, they do not trust the courts to hold the gates open very long. There may be that time again when the unempowered will be completely at the mercy of the schools.

Finally, if we are not careful, literacy may be misconstrued as the measure of a human being's worth. We could end up using literacy to separate the goats, who will be expected to go down into the pit of outer darkness, where there will be weeping and gnashing of teeth, from the sheep, who expect to inherit the earth. In such a time, literacy as a human problem will no longer be at issue; the question will be, What is human?

Dallas, Texas

Notes

1. *Brown* v. *Board of Education of Topeka*, 347 U.S. 483, 74 S.Ct. 686, 98 L. Ed. 873.

2. *Lau* v. *Nichols*, 414 U.S. 563, 94 S.Ct. 786, 39 L. Ed. 2d. 1 (1974).

3. *Debra P.* v. *Turlington*, D.Ct. Fla., 474 F. Supp. 244.

4. *Martin Luther King, Junior, Elementary School Children et al.* v. *Ann Arbor School District Board*, 473 F. Supp. 1371, D.Ct. Mich., 1979.

5. Theodore James Pinnock (in consultation with A. P. Torrence et al.), *Results of an Exploratory Study of Functional Illiterates in Macon County, Alabama* (Tuskegee, Alabama: Tuskegee Institute, 1966).

6. *San Antonio Independent School District* v. *Rodriguez*, 411 U.S. 1, 93 S.Ct. 1278, 36 L. Ed. 2d 16 (1973).

7. Daniel P. Resnick and Lauren B. Resnick, "The Nature of Literacy: A Historical Exploration," *Harvard Educational Review* 47 (August 1977): 370–85.

8. Leon Botstein, "A Proper Education," *Harper's*, September 1979, pp. 33–37.

9. Mina Shaughnessy, *Errors and Expectations: A Guide for the Teacher of Basic Writing* (New York: Oxford University Press, 1977).

Why Good English Is Good for You

JOHN SIMON

John Simon is well known to readers of New York *magazine as a drama critic, and to readers of the* National Review *as a film critic, and to readers of* Esquire *(before it changed hands) as a language critic. He is well known to all his readers as a writer of exquisitely precise prose, barbed with acerbic wit. He knows the English language from the outside as well as from within, having been born in Yugoslavia, but later immigrating to the United States and receiving his A.B., M.A., and Ph.D. from Harvard University.*

The essay he read at The University of Alabama's Symposium on Literacy has since been published with other essays in Paradigms Lost *(New York: Clarkson N. Potter, 1980). It is reprinted here because, like many journalists, Simon considers the linguistic philosophy expressed elsewhere in this volume to be antithetical to the best interests of language, letters, and the humanistic tradition.*

What's good English to you that, though it may be subjected to as many grievances as were Hecuba and Niobe combined, you should grieve for it? What good is correct speech and writing, you may ask, in an age in which hardly anyone seems to know, and no one seems to care? Why shouldn't you just fling bloopers, bloopers riotously with the throng, and not stick out from the rest like a sore thumb by using the language correctly? Isn't grammar really a thing of the past, and isn't the new idea to communicate in *any* way as long as you can make yourself understood?

Let us, for a moment, go back into the past, or, to be as nearly exact as I can, to the early 1630s, when Etienne Pascal was teaching his barely teenaged son, Blaise, about languages. As Blaise's elder sister, Gilberte, was to report in a memoir later on, the father was making "him perceive in general what languages were about; he showed him how they were reduced to grammars subject to certain rules; that these rules had yet some exceptions that had been carefully noted; and that means had thus been found to make languages communicable from country to country. This general idea disentangled his mind"—or, as some of you today might put it, *blew* his mind; in the original, "lui débrouillait l'esprit." All this Etienne taught Blaise *before* he was twelve, at which time he started him out on his first foreign language, which was Latin.

Let us now take an even longer step back, to 1511, in which year Erasmus's *The Praise of Folly* was published. In this facetious, satirical work, Folly herself is speaking (I quote only brief excerpts, in H. H. Hudson's translation): "Among those who maintain . . . an appearance of wisdom," she declares, "the grammarians hold first place." Their schools are "knowledge factories . . . mills . . . even . . . shambles." "Yet thanks to me," Folly continues, "they see themselves as the first among men," beating the living daylights out of their wretched students, whom "they cram . . . with utter nonsense." The grammarians are particularly delighted when they "can drag out of some worm-eaten manuscript . . . some word not generally known," or some other trivial information; they also form mutual admiration societies, "scratching each other's itch. Yet if one commits a lapse in a single

word, and another . . . lights on it . . . what a stir presently, what scufflings, what insults." Then Folly cites a
certain polymath who laid aside all other pursuits to hurl
himself into the study of grammar so as to settle at last
issues that "none of the Greeks or Latins succeeded in
doing definitively. It becomes a matter to be put to the
test of battle when someone makes a conjunction of a
word which belongs in the bailiwick of adverbs. Thanks
to him, there are as many grammars as there are grammarians—nay, more," and Folly names the great printer
Aldus, who published at least five different books on
grammar.

Here we have the two extremes: in Erasmus, grammar
ridiculed as the ultimate waste of both students' and
teachers' time; in Gilberte Pascal's memoir of her brother,
the principles of grammar shown as the abolishers of
boundaries between countries and the clearers of a young
mind. I think both statements are as true today as they
were then, but both, of course, are to some extent over-
simplifications. The virtues of grammar—or, in our case,
of good English—are not quite so monolithically man-
ifest as all that; nor is the pigheaded, despotic nit-picking
of the perfectionists, elitists, or fuddy-duddies (call them
what you will) entirely misguided and ludicrous.

The usual, basic defense of good English (and here,
again, let us not worry about nomenclature—for all I
care, you may call it "standard English," "correct American," or anything else) is that it helps communication,
that it is perhaps even a *sine qua non* of mutual understanding. Although this is a crude truth of sorts, it
strikes me as, in some ways, both more and less than the
truth. Suppose you say, "Everyone in their right mind
would cross on the green light" or "Hopefully, it won't
rain tomorrow," chances are very good that the person
you say this to will understand you, even though you are

committing obvious solecisms or creating needless ambiguities. Similarly, if you write in a letter, "The baby has finally ceased it's howling," the recipient will be able to figure out what was meant. But "figuring out" is precisely what a listener or reader should not have to do. There is, of course, the fundamental matter of courtesy to the other person, but it goes beyond that: why waste time on unscrambling simple meaning when there are more complex questions that should receive our undivided attention? If the many cooks had to worry first about which out of a large number of pots had no leak in it, the broth, whether spoiled or not, would take forever to be ready.

It is, I repeat, only initially a matter of clarity. It is also a matter of concision. Space today is as limited as time. If you have only a thousand words in which to convey an important message it helps to know that "overcomplicated" is correct and "overly complicated" is incorrect. Never mind the grammatical explanations; the two extra characters and one space between words are reason enough. But what about the more advanced forms of word-mongering that hold sway nowadays? Take redundancy, like the "hopes and aspirations" of Jimmy Carter, quoted by Edwin Newman as having "a deeply profound religious experience"; or elaborate jargon, as when Charles G. Walcutt, a graduate professor of English at CUNY, writes (again as quoted by Newman): "The colleges, trying to remediate increasing numbers of . . . illiterates up to college levels, are being highschoolized"; or just obfuscatory verbiage of the pretentious sort, such as this fragment from a letter I received: "It is my impression that effective *inter*personal verbal communication depends on prior effective *intra*-personal verbal communication." What this means is that if you think clearly, you can speak and write clearly—except if you are a "certified speech and language pathologist," like the writer of the letter I quote. (By the way, she adds the letters Ph.D. after her name, though she is not even from Germany, where *Herr* and *Frau Doktor* are in common, not to say vulgar, use.)

But except for her ghastly verbiage, our certified language pathologist (whatever that means) is perfectly right: there is a close connection between the ability to think and the ability to use English correctly. After all, we think in words, we conceptualize in words, we work out our problems inwardly with words, and using them correctly is comparable to a craftsman's treating his tools with care, keeping his materials in good shape. Would you trust a weaver who hangs her wet laundry on her loom, or lets her cats bed down in her yarn? The person who does not respect words and their proper relationships cannot have much respect for ideas at all. My quarrel is not so much with minor errors that we all fall into from time to time even if we know better as it is with basic sloppiness or ignorance or defiance of good English.

Training yourself to speak and write correctly—and I say "training yourself" because nowadays, unfortunately, you cannot depend on other people or on institutions to give you the proper training, for reasons I shall discuss later—training yourself, then, in language, means developing at the very least two extremely useful faculties: your sense of discipline and your memory. Discipline because language is with us always, as nothing else is: it follows us much as, in the old morality play, Good Deeds followed Everyman, all the way to the grave; and, if the language is written, even beyond. Let me explain: if you can keep an orderly apartment, if you can see to it that your correspondence and bill-paying are attended to regularly, if your diet and wardrobe are maintained with the necessary care—good enough; you are a disciplined person.

But the preliminary discipline underlying all others is nevertheless your speech: the words that come out of you almost as frequently and—if you are tidy—as regularly as your breath. I would go so far as to say that, immediately after your bodily functions, language is first, unless you happen to be an ascetic, an anchorite, or a stylite; but unless you are a styl*ite,* you had better be a styl*ist.*

Most of us—almost all—must take in and give out language as we do breath, and we had better consider the seriousness of language pollution as second only to air pollution. For the linguistically disciplined, to misuse or mispronounce a word is an unnecessary and unhealthy contribution to the surrounding smog. To have taught ourselves not to do this, or—being human and thus also imperfect—to do it as little as possible, means deriving from every speaking moment the satisfaction we get from a cap that snaps on to a container perfectly, an elevator that stops flush with the landing, a roulette ball that comes to rest exactly on the number on which we have placed our bet. It gives us the pleasure of hearing or seeing our words—because they are abiding by the rules—snapping, sliding, falling precisely into place, expressing with perfect lucidity and symmetry just what we wanted them to express. This is comparable to the satisfaction of the athlete or ballet dancer or pianist finding his body or legs or fingers doing his bidding with unimpeachable accuracy.

And if someone now says that "in George Eliot's lesser novels, she is not completely in command" is perfectly comprehensible even if it is ungrammatical, the "she" having no antecedent in the nominative (*Eliot's* is a genitive), I say, "Comprehensible, perhaps, but lopsided," for the civilized and orderly mind does not feel comfortable with that "she"—does not hear that desired and satisfying click of correctness—unless the sentence is restruc-

tured as "George Eliot, in her lesser novels, is not . . ." or
in some similar way. In fact, the fully literate ear can be
thrown by this error in syntax; it may look for the antecedent of that "she" elsewhere than in the preceding posses-
sive case. Be that as it may, playing without rules and
winning—in this instance, managing to communicate
without using good English—is no more satisfactory
than winning in a sport or game by accident or by dis-
regarding the rules: which is really cheating.

The second faculty good speech develops is, as I have
mentioned before, our memory. Grammar and syntax are
partly logical—and to that extent they are also good
exercisers and developers of our logical faculty—but they
are also partly arbitrary, conventional, irrational. For
example, the correct "compared to" and "contrasted
with" could, from the logical point of view, just as well be
"contrasted to" and "compared with" ("compared with,"
of course, is correct, but in a different sense from the one
that concerns us here, namely, the antithesis of "contrasted with"). And, apropos *different,* logic would have
to strain desperately to explain the exclusive correctness
of "other than," which would seem to justify "different
than," jarring though that is to the cultivated ear.

But there it is: some things are so because tradition,
usage, the best speakers and writers, the grammar
books, and dictionaries have made them so. There may
even exist some hidden historical explanation: something, perhaps, in the Sanskrit, Greek, Latin, or other
origins of a word or construction that you and I may very
easily never know. We can, however, memorize; and memorization can be a wonderfully useful thing—surely the
Greeks were right to consider Mnemosyne (memory) the
mother of the Muses, for without her there would be no
art and no science. And what better place to practice one's
mnemonic skills than in the study of one's language?

There is something particularly useful about speaking correctly and precisely because language is always there as a foundation—or, if you prefer a more fluid image, an undercurrent—beneath what is going on. Now, it seems to me that the great difficulty of life lies in the fact that we must almost always do two things at a time. If, for example, we are walking and conversing, we must keep our mouths as well as feet from stumbling. If we are driving while listening to music, we must not allow the siren song of the cassette to prevent us from watching the road and the speedometer (otherwise the less endearing siren of the police car or the ambulance will follow apace). Well, it is just this sort of bifurcation of attention that care for precise, clear expression fosters in us. By learning early in life to pay attention both to what we are saying and to how we are saying it, we develop the much-needed life skill of doing two things simultaneously.

Put another way, we foster our awareness of, and ability to deal with, form and content. If there is any verity that modern criticism has fought for, it is the recognition of the indissolubility of content and form. Criticism won the battle, won it so resoundingly that this oneness has become a contemporary commonplace. And shall the fact that form is content be a platitude in all the arts but go unrecognized in the art of self-expression, whether in conversation or correspondence, or whatever form of spoken or written utterance a human being resorts to? Accordingly, you are going to be judged, whether you like it or not, by the correctness of your English as much as by the correctness of your thinking; there are some people to whose ear bad English is as offensive as gibberish, or as your picking your nose in public would be to their eyes and stomachs. The fact that people of linguistic sensibilities may be a dying breed does not mean that they are wholly extinct, and it is best not to take any unnecessary chances.

To be sure, if you are a member of a currently favored minority, many of your linguistic failings may be forgiven you—whether rightly or wrongly is not my concern here. But if you cannot change your sex or color to the one that is getting preferential treatment—Bakke case or no Bakke case—you might as well learn good English and profit by it in your career, your social relations, perhaps even in your basic self-confidence. That, if you will, is the ultimate practical application of good English; but now let me tell you about the ultimate impractical one, which strikes me as being possibly even more important.

Somewhere in the prose writings of Charles Péguy, who was a very fine poet and prose writer—and, what is perhaps even more remarkable, as good a human being as he was an artist—somewhere in those writings is a passage about the decline of pride in workmanship among French artisans, which, as you can deduce, set in even before World War I, wherein Péguy was killed. In the passage I refer to, Péguy bemoans the fact that cabinetmakers no longer finish the backs of furniture—the sides that go against the wall—in the same way as they do the exposed sides. What is not seen was just as important to the old artisans as what is seen—it was a moral issue with them. And so, I think, it ought to be with language. Even if no one else notices the niceties, the precision, the impeccable sense of grammar and syntax you deploy in your utterances, you yourself should be aware of them and take pride in them as in pieces of work well done.

Now, I realize that there are two possible reactions among you to what I have said up to this point. Some of you will say to yourselves, What utter nonsense! Language is a flexible, changing, living organism that belongs to the people who speak it. It has always been changed according to the ways in which people chose to speak it, and the dictionaries and books on grammar had to, and will have to, adjust themselves to the people and not the other way around. For isn't it the glory of language that it keeps throwing up new inventions as surf tosses out differently polished pebbles and bits of bottle glass onto the shore, and that in this inexhaustible variety, in this refusal to kowtow to dry-as-dust scholars, lies its vitality, its beauty?

Others among you, perhaps fewer in number, will say to yourselves: quite so, there is such a thing as standard English, or purity of speech, or correctness of expression—something worth safeguarding and fostering; but how the devil is one to accomplish that under the prevailing conditions: in a democratic society full of minorities that have their own dialects or linguistic preferences, and in a world in which television, advertising, and other mass media manage daily to corrupt the language a little further? Let me try to answer the first group first, and then come back to the questions of the second.

Of course language is, and must be, a living organism to the extent that new inventions, discoveries, ideas, enter the scene and clamor rightfully for designations. Political, social, and psychological changes may also affect our mode of expression, and new words or phrases may have to be found to reflect what we might call historical changes. It is also quite natural for slang terms to be invented, become popular, and, in some cases, remain permanently in the language. It is perhaps equally inevitable (though here we are on more speculative ground) for certain words to become obsolescent and obsolete, and drop out of the language. But does that mean that grammar and syntax have to keep changing, that pronunciations and meanings of words must shift, that more complex or elegant forms are obliged to yield to simpler or cruder ones that often are not fully synonymous with them and not capable of expressing certain fine distinctions? Should, for instance, *terrestrial* disappear entirely in favor of *earthly,* or are there shades of meaning involved that need to remain available to us? Must we sacrifice *notwithstanding* because we have *in spite of* or *despite*? Need we forfeit *jettison* just because we have *throw overboard*? And what about *disinterested,* which is becoming a synonym for *uninterested,* even though that means something else, and though we have no other word for *disinterested*?

"Language has *always* changed," say these people, and they might with equal justice say that there has always been war or sickness or insanity. But the truth is that some sicknesses that formerly killed millions have been eliminated, that some so-called insanity can today be treated, and that just because there have always been wars does not mean that someday a cure cannot be found even for that scourge. And if it cannot, it is only by striving to put an absolute end to war, by pretending that it can be licked, that we can at least partly control it. Without such assumptions and efforts, the evil would be so widespread that, given our current weaponry, we would no longer be here to worry about the future of language.

But we are here, and having evolved linguistically this far, and having the means—books of grammar, dictionaries, education for all—to arrest unnecessary change, why not endeavor with might and main to arrest it? Certain cataclysms cannot be prevented: earthquakes and droughts, for example, can scarcely, if at all, be controlled; but we can prevent floods, for which purpose we have invented dams. And dams are precisely what we can construct to prevent floods of ignorance from eroding our language, and, beyond that, to provide irrigation for areas that would otherwise remain linguistically arid.

For consider that what some people are pleased to call linguistic evolution was almost always a matter of ignorance prevailing over knowledge. There is no valid reason, for example, for the word *nice* to have changed its meaning so many times—except ignorance of its exact definition. Had the change never occurred, or had it been stopped at any intermediate stage, we would have had just as good a word as we have now and saved some people a heap of confusion along the way. But if *nice* means what it does today—and it has two principal meanings, one of them, as in "nice distinction," alas, obsolescent—let us, for heaven's sake, keep it where it is, now that we have the means with which to hold it there.

If, for instance, we lose the accusative case *whom*—and we are in great danger of losing it—our language will be the poorer for it. Obviously, "The man, whom I had never known, was a thief" means something other than "The man who I had never known was a thief." Now, you can object that it would be just as easy in the first instance to use some other construction; but what happens if *this* one is used incorrectly? Ambiguity and confusion. And why should we lose this useful distinction? Just because a million or ten million or a billion people less educated than we are cannot master the difference? Surely it behooves us to try to educate the ignorant up to our level rather than to stultify ourselves down to theirs. Yes, you say, but suppose they refuse to or are unable to learn? In that case, I say, there is a doubly good reason for not going along with them. Ah, you reply, but they are the majority, and we must accept their way or, if the revolution is merely linguistic, lose our "credibility" (as the current parlance, rather confusingly, has it), or, if the revolution is political, lose our heads. Well, I consider a sufficient number of people to be educable enough to be capable of using *who* and *whom* correctly, and to derive satisfaction from this capability—a sufficient number, I mean, to enable us to preserve *whom*, and not to have to ask "for who the bell tolls."

The main problem with education, actually, is not those who need it and cannot get it, but those who should impart it and, for various reasons, do not. In short, the enemies of education are the educators themselves: mis-educated, underpaid, overburdened, and intimidated teachers (frightened because, though the pen is supposed to be mightier than the sword, the switchblade is surely more powerful than the ferule), and professors who—because they are structural linguists, democratic respec-ters of alleged minority rights, or otherwise misguided folk—believe in the sacrosanct privilege of any culturally underprivileged minority or majority to dictate its igno-rance to the rest of the world. For, I submit, an English improvised by slaves and other strangers to the culture—to whom my heart goes out in every human way—under dreadfully deprived conditions can nowise equal an Eng-lish that the best literary and linguistic talents have, over the centuries, perceptively and painstakingly brought to a high level of excellence.

So my answer to the scoffers in this or any audience is, in simplest terms, the following: contrary to popular misconception, language does not belong to the people, or at least not in the sense in which *belong* is usually con-strued. For things can rightfully belong only to those who invent or earn them. But we do not know who invented language: is it the people who first made up the words for *father* and *mother,* for *I* and *thou,* for *hand* and *foot;* or is it the people who evolved the subtler shadings of language, its poetic variety and suggestiveness, but also its unambiguousness, its accurate and telling details? Those are two very different groups of people and two very different languages, and I, as you must have guessed by now, consider the latter group at least as important as the former. As for *earning* language, it has surely been earned by those who have striven to learn it properly, and here even economic and social circumstances are but an imperfect excuse for bad usage; history is full of examples of people rising from humble origins to learn, against all kinds of odds, to speak and write correctly—even brilliantly.

Belong, then, should be construed in the sense that parks, national forests, monuments, and public utilities are said to belong to the people: available for properly respectful use but not for defacement and destruction. And all that we propose to teach is how to use and enjoy the gardens of language to their utmost aesthetic and salubrious potential. Still, I must now address myself to the group that, while agreeing with my aims, despairs of finding practical methods for their implementation.

True enough, after a certain age speakers not aware of standard English or not exceptionally gifted will find it hard or impossible to change their ways. Nevertheless, if there were available funds for advanced methods in teaching; if teachers themselves were better trained and paid, and had smaller classes and more assistants; if, furthermore, college entrance requirements were heightened and the motivation of students accordingly strengthened; if there were no structural linguists and National Councils of Teachers of English filling instructors' heads with notions about "Students' Rights to Their Own Language" (they have every right to it as a second language, but none as a first); if teachers in all disciplines, including the sciences and social sciences, graded on English usage as well as on specific proficiencies; if aptitude tests for various jobs stressed good English more than they do; and, above all, if parents were better educated and more aware of the need to set a good example to their children, and to encourage them to learn correct usage, the situation could improve enormously.

Clearly, to expect all this to come to pass is utopian; some of it, however, is well within the realm of possibility. For example, even if parents do not speak very good English, many of them at least can manage an English that is good enough to correct a very young child's mistakes; in other words, most adults can speak a good enough four-year-old's idiom. They would thus start kids out on the right path; the rest could be done by the schools.

But the problem is what to do in the most underprivileged homes: those of blacks, Hispanics, immigrants from various Asian and European countries. This is where day-care centers could come in. If the fathers and mothers could be gainfully employed, their small children would be looked after by day-care centers where—is this asking too much?—good English could be inculcated in them. The difficulty, of course, is what to do about the discrepancy the little ones would note between the speech of the day-care people and that of their parents. Now, it seems to me that small children have a far greater ability to learn things, including languages, than some people give them credit for. Much of it is indeed rote learning, but, where languages are concerned, that is one of the basic learning methods even for adults. There is no reason for not teaching kids another language, to wit, standard English, and turning this, if desirable, into a game: "At home you speak one way; here we have another language," at which point the instructor can make up names and explanations for standard English that would appeal to pupils of that particular place, time, and background.

At this stage of the game, as well as later on in school,

care should be exercised to avoid insulting the language spoken in the youngsters' homes. There must be ways to convey that both home and school languages have their validity and uses and that knowing both enables one to accomplish more in life. This would be hard to achieve if the children's parents were, say, militant blacks of the Geneva Smitherman sort, who execrate standard English as a weapon of capitalist oppression against the poor of all races, colors, and religions. But, happily, there is evidence that most black, Hispanic, and other nonstandard English–speaking parents want their children to learn correct English so as to get ahead in the world.

Yet how do we defend ourselves against the charge that we are old fogeys who cannot emotionally adjust to the new directions an ever-living and changing language must inevitably take? Here I would want to redefine or, at any rate, clarify, what "living and changing" means, and also explain where we old fogeys stand. Misinformed attacks on Old Fogeydom, I have noticed, invariably represent us as people who shudder at a split infinitive and would sooner kill or be killed than tolerate a sentence that ends with a preposition. Actually, despite all my travels through Old Fogeydom, I have yet to meet one inhabitant who would not stick a preposition onto the tail of a sentence; as for splitting infinitives, most of us O.F.'s are perfectly willing to do that, too, but tactfully and sparingly, where it feels right. There is no earthly reason, for example, for saying "to dangerously live," when "to live dangerously" sounds so much better; but it does seem right to say (and write) "What a delight to sweetly breathe in your sleeping lover's breath"; that sounds smoother, indeed sweeter, than "to breathe in sweetly" or "sweetly to breathe in." But infinitives begging to be split are relatively rare. A sensitive ear, a good eye for shades of meaning will alert you whenever the need to split arises; without that ear and eye, you had better stick to the rules.

About the sense in which language is, and must be, alive, let me speak while donning another of my several hats—actually it is not a hat but a cap, for there exists in Greenwich Village an inscription on a factory that reads "CRITIC CAPS." So with my drama critic's cap on, let me present you with an analogy. The world theater today is full of directors who wreak havoc on classic plays to demonstrate their own ingenuity, their superiority, as it were, to the author. These directors—aborted playwrights, for the most part—will stage productions of *Hamlet* in which the prince is a woman, a flaming homosexual, or a one-eyed hunchback.

Well, it seems to me that the same spirit prevails in our approach to linguistics, with every newfangled, ill-informed, know-nothing construction, definition, pronunciation enshrined by the joint efforts of structural linguists, permissive dictionaries, and allegedly democratic but actually demagogic educators. What really makes a production of, say, *Hamlet* different, and therefore alive, is that the director, while trying to get as faithfully as possible at Shakespeare's meanings, nevertheless ends up stressing things in the play that strike him most forcefully; and the same individuality in production design and performances (the Hamlet of Gielgud versus the Hamlet of Olivier, for instance—what a world of difference!) further differentiates one production from another, and bestows on each its particular vitality. So, too, language remains alive because each speaker (or writer) can and must, *within the framework of accepted grammar, syntax, and pronunciation,* produce a style that is his very own, that is as personal as his posture, way of walking, mode of dress, and so on. It is such stylistic differences that make a person's—or a nation's—language flavorous, pungent, alive, and all this without having to play fast and loose with the existing rules.

But to have this, we need, among other things, good teachers and, beyond them, enlightened educators. I shudder when I read in the *Birmingham* (Alabama) *Post-Herald* of October 6, 1978, an account of a talk given to eight hundred English teachers by Dr. Alan C. Purves, vice-president of the National Council of Teachers of English. Dr. Purves is quoted as saying things like "We are in a situation with respect to reading where . . . ," and culminating in the following truly horrifying sentence: "I am going to suggest that when we go back to the basics, I think what we should be dealing with is our charge to help students to be more proficient in producing meaningful language—language that says what it means." Notice all the deadwood, the tautology, the anacoluthon in the first part of that sentence; but notice especially the absurdity of the latter part, in which the dubious word *meaningful*—a poor relation of *significant*—is thought to require explaining to an audience of English teachers.

Given such leadership from the N.C.T.E., the time must be at hand when we shall hear—not just, "Don't ask for who the bell rings" (*ask not* and *tolls* being, of course, archaic, elitist language), but also, "It rings for you and I."

Language: Unites or Divides? The Students' Right in Retrospect

ELISABETH McPHERSON

As a teacher, author, administrator, and leader, Elisabeth McPherson has been at the forefront of a movement to bring linguistic scholarship to bear upon the teaching of English in American schools and colleges. She was one of the most outspoken advocates for a controversial resolution, "The Students' Right to Their Own Language," when it was passed in 1974 at the national convention of the Conference on College Composition and Communication. In this essay, McPherson reflects on the attitudes and misapprehensions that continue to cause the resolution to be misunderstood even today, more than six years after it was passed. She argues that genuine respect for the language spoken by minority children in their homes and neighborhoods is not only compatible with the English teacher's traditional objectives, but may even be essential to establishing the atmosphere in which these objectives can be achieved.

When I produced the title of this paper, almost off the top of my head as usual, it seemed pretty clear to me that if all of us—parents, teachers, and that imaginary creation known as THE PUBLIC—forgot for awhile about the differences in the way we use our language and concentrated instead on the similarities, we'd take a big step toward using language to unite us. After all, the similarities far outweigh the minor differences. If that were not so, we couldn't understand each other, and I think nobody much denies that we *can* understand, if we try. It's not misunderstanding that divides us, it's disapproval. We let language divide us when we insist that one way of saying something is always WRONG, another way is always RIGHT, and that the people who make the same choices we make are brighter, more valuable, more worth knowing, and, though we seldom say it quite that crudely, somehow better people.

I realized a little later that the title was easy to misinterpret. Some people may suppose that language divides us when we do make different choices, that the only way language can really unite us is for the schools to keep on doggedly trying, as we have been unsuccessfully trying for years and years, to make all Americans talk like a textbook. I'd better begin by saying that I disagree strongly with that position. I don't want everybody to sound the same. Even if it could be done, it would be dreadfully dull. More important, I don't want us to keep trying, because the more effort we spend on trying to eradicate differences, the less effort we spend on the real business of English teachers—helping all students to read with understanding, talk with confidence, and write with clarity, and helping students accomplish those three aims with the pleasure that should accompany them rather than the pain that so often does.

It was with those ideas in mind that, nearly six years ago, the Conference on College Composition and Communication issued its statement on the students' right to their own language. That statement, about which I assume most people have at least heard, was accompanied by eighteen small-print pages of background and thir-

teen even smaller-print pages of bibliography. The book-
let, put together by a committee of linguists and teachers, was read, I suspect, by those already committed to
language diversity and ignored by the purists who believe the main business of English teachers should be
chasing mistakes. CCCC, being neither naïve nor sim-
pleminded, expected the statement to be controversial,
but perhaps it did not realize quite what a furious attack
the six sentences of the resolution would arouse, both
inside and outside the profession.

A few angry traditionalists canceled their membership
in the organization. Newspapers and magazines, almost
without exception, denounced and ridiculed the statement. People expressed their outrage without bothering
to find out why the resolution had passed, and without
much logic. They reacted as though the first sentence
("We affirm the students' right to their own patterns and
varieties of language—the dialects of their nurture or
whatever dialects in which they find their own identity
and style") meant that teachers were deliberately denying students a chance to practice other patterns and
varieties of English. They assumed that students who
used their own dialects could not increase their vocabu-
laries, in spite of the fact that speakers of any dialect can
learn new words whenever the words are needed. They
assumed we were *teaching* street language, slang, and
vulgarities, in spite of the fact that the term *dialect* refers
to a fixed set of minor differences in pronunciation, syntax, and usage, in spite of the fact that everybody speaks a
dialect.

They read the sentence as if it had an *only* in it: "Students have a right *only* to the language they learned as
infants," as if a right to one thing automatically excluded
rights to anything else. Such critics seemed to believe
that English teaching meant error-chasing and no more,

an impression perhaps derived from the misery of their own experiences at school, and that English teachers who didn't spend their time clobbering so-called mistakes were doing nothing at all. Teachers who defended the "Students' Right" statement were accused of dereliction of duty, of baby-sitting, of perpetrating a fraud, of accepting money under false pretenses, of cheating the public that paid them.

Actually, that first sentence says more about the rights *teachers* should *not* have. Teachers have no right to belittle students for their speech habits, or to hold their home dialects up to scorn, or even to try to eradicate those dialects. The sentence means that teachers should live up to what we all know—that the purpose of language is communication—and when teachers really don't understand what their pupils are saying, the teachers should ask real questions. Above all, it means that teachers must respect the language skills students bring with them.

It's not just teachers who must show such respect and such understanding. Everybody connected with a school needs to do it, including administrators. Leslie Whipp, writing in the May 1979 issue of *College Composition and Communication,* tells what happened in a junior high math class in a school where most of the students spoke both Spanish and English. When one little girl solved a math problem correctly, speaking in Spanish, the supervisor who was observing the class interrupted to say that the students must talk English, whereupon the child burst into tears and wouldn't recite again. Fortunately the teacher, as Whipp comments, was not one to confuse ends—learning mathematics—with means—displaying linguistic status. As soon as the supervisor left, the teacher went back to letting the children learn arithmetic in the language that made them comfortable, and the little girl, presumably, was not turned off math in the way that a lot of children are turned against reading and writing.

The second sentence of the CCCC resolution said that "language scholars long ago denied that the myth of a standard American dialect has any validity." There wasn't much angry outcry over that one, perhaps because the people most incensed by the resolution weren't very sure what language scholars had been saying and they didn't want to display their lack of information. Rather than arguing the point, they ignored it and went right on talking about "standard English," which they didn't consider a dialect at all. Standard English, according to who was protesting, could mean either of two things: it could refer to the way they talked themselves, or it could refer to the way they wished they talked, but didn't. The latter group attributed their failure, of course, to some terrible shortcoming in themselves and remained convinced that a real standard speech existed somewhere, like pie in the sky, and it was the school's business to force-feed it.

Rather than a single standard American speech, there are a number of acceptable American dialects, and their acceptability depends on where you are, whom you're talking to, and what you're talking about. The sounds I hear on a university campus in Alabama are not the sounds I hear at home in Washington, and neither of these are the sounds I'd hear if I went to New England. The jargon at a meeting of the American Medical Association differs from the jargon of the American Bar Association, and neither is much like the jargon at a conference on literacy. It should go without saying that none of these ways of talking much resembles the way these same people will talk when they get safely home.

The third sentence of the resolution says, "The claim that any one dialect is unacceptable amounts to an attempt of one social group to exert its dominance over another." That one has not been much discussed either. Critics perfer to talk in terms of right and wrong, rather than in terms of power and powerlessness, prestige and poverty. But variations don't seem to matter when they're regional or professional; it's the economic or social or ethnic variations that offend.

What those who condemn the language habits of people whose backgrounds differ from their own are actually doing is trying to maintain their own sense of social superiority. What teachers who condemn those habits are actually doing is exercising a kind of linguistic censorship, a censorship just as damaging to the cause of genuine literacy as the recent Island Tree decision in New York. In that case, five high school students filed suit in a federal district court against the Island Tree School Board for removing eleven books from the school library. In deciding against the students, the judge said that although he believed removing the books reflected a "misguided educational philosophy," the removal was "within the broad range of discretion [granted] to educational officials . . . elected by the community." Counsel for the Civil Liberties Union, which acted for the students, said the case brought into focus the question of whether books can be banned for political, religious, and cultural reasons. The attorney for the board said it was a school board's "duty to reflect community values—to indoctrinate community values."

The parallel between censoring books, which most of us would oppose, I presume, and censoring language variations seems to me obvious. Both kinds of censorship are based on political and cultural values. The students in New York will probably appeal their case. They'll get help from various professional organizations who do not believe the right to read should be curtailed by a small group of people, even though they are elected, just because that small group doesn't want students to know what it was like to grow up as an Indian *(Laughing Boy)*, or a Puerto Rican *(Down These Mean Streets)*, or a Jew *(The Fixer)*, or a black (the writings of Eldridge Cleaver and Langston Hughes). The "Students' Right" resolution was—and still is—an appeal against the censorship of language, an appeal made on behalf of the people the Long Island school board doesn't want their students to know about.

The fourth sentence of the CCCC statement said, "Such a claim [that any one dialect is unacceptable] leads to false advice for speakers and writers, and immoral advice for humans." That part of the statement was attacked within the profession, not by the press, on the grounds that *immoral* was too strong a term. The false advice part didn't get much attention. No speaker is limited to one way of talking to every listener on every occasion. Even very young children are adept at adjusting their language choices. They don't talk to their contemporaries the way they talk to adults; they don't talk to strangers the way they talk to their parents. And effective writers are skillful in varying their styles. They know that the dialect suitable to a business letter would sound strange in a poem, that the dialect fitting the needs of poetry won't do for an argument either for or against standardized testing. To deny what we know to be so, in real communication outside of school, does seem to me immoral—and it's even more immoral to use that false advice to make people feel inferior.

The fifth sentence reads: "A nation proud of its diverse heritage and its cultural and racial variety will preserve its heritage of dialects." I'm not so sure any more that most of us are proud of our diverse heritage, although it has been fashionable for the last few years to pretend that we are. But whether or not we want to preserve our heritage of dialects, a lot of schools are still using teaching strategies developed when the melting-pot theory was in style. Fifty or sixty years ago European immigrants didn't want to remember their origins, they wanted to conceal them. Their children were encouraged to forget the foreign languages they heard at home and master idiomatic English as fast as they could. But the attitudes and approaches that worked well for people learning a second language are not the approaches and attitudes that will help native speakers enlarge their language capacities, whatever dialects they speak.

Native speakers come to school with the basic grammar of the language built into them—"basic grammar" in the linguistic, rather than the popular sense of the term. Linguistically, *grammar* means the way in which a language transfers meaning beyond the meaning of individual words by themselves. Although English contains some inflections—changes in words that show differences in number or time (child, children; house, houses; was, were; bite, bit; want, wanted, for instance)— it is primarily a word-order language. The two sentences, "The dog bit the man," and "The man bit the dog," are vastly different in meaning, even though the five words in both sentences are exactly the same. The distinction is not in vocabulary but in the grammar that is built into us.

The various ways in which the term *grammar* is used are responsible for much of the confusion about language teaching. More than twenty-five years ago Nelson Francis distinguished three meanings, which he called Grammar I, Grammar II, and Grammar III. Grammar I is the way the language operates, the system all native speakers learn when they begin to talk, the difference between "Dog bites man" and "Man bites dog." Grammar II is the analysis of that system: the explanation that *man* is a noun, *bite* is a verb, *bit* is a verb in the past tense, and that in the majority of English sentences, the noun that precedes the verb is doing something, the noun that comes after the verb is having something done to it. The three-year-old who says, "The man bited the dog," is perfectly aware of who did the biting, and so is everybody else who hears that sentence, even though the child has not yet learned that the grammatical rule, adding the inflection -*ed* indicates an event in the past, doesn't work for all English verbs, and is certainly unaware that *bite* is a verb.

When that same child gets a little older and is asked in school to find the verb and diagram the sentence, the child is being taught Grammar II, the identification and classification of what is already a built-in system. But learning to call "man" the subject of the sentence and "bit the dog" the predicate has no more to do with the ability to speak and understand than learning the names of the muscles and bones in their bodies has to do with children's ability to walk and run. Grammar II is the scientific study of human language behavior, not the behavior itself.

Grammar III is what linguists call usage. It's the difference between the three-year-old's "bited" and the older child's "bit," between "Dick is going" and "Dick be going," between "haven't any" and "ain't got no." It's what people mean when they say, "John Smith's an English teacher; you'd better watch your grammar." They don't mean John won't understand you if you say, "My wife and me bought a new house"; they do mean John will probably disapprove of you, just as he might disapprove if you went barefoot to church. It's a matter of etiquette, not a matter of comprehension.

Different English dialects follow different rules, and those rules, like the rest of the basic grammar they know, are learned automatically by small children as they learn to speak. In some varieties of black English, "be going" rather than "is going" is a rule—a regular and required way of indicating a subtle difference in meaning. In some dialects of English, difference in time needs to be shown only once, rather than twice as so-called standard English requires. In the sentence, "Yesterday our house burn down," it's just as clear that the burning occurred in the past as it is in the more conventional "Yesterday our house burn*ed* down." If we're really interested in understanding, if we care more about the homeless family than about the etiquette of language, we'll respond, not to the missing -*ed* but to the tragedy of the fire. If we're really interested in diversity, we'll talk about how interesting these minor variations are and the different impressions they create, but we won't use the variations to divide the so-called good from the so-called bad.

The final sentence of the "Students' Right" statement is the most vital in promoting real literacy for all students, and it has been the least discussed and the least observed. That sentence reads: "We affirm strongly that teachers must have the experiences and training that will enable them to respect diversity and uphold the right of students to their own language." Most English teachers know a lot about literature and very little about the nature of language. The midwestern university English department that told my daughter ten years ago that taking linguistics was a waste of time—she'd do better to concentrate on the eighteenth century—is still giving the same advice. I don't mean to sound antiliterature or anticulture. The study of literature should be a joy, and writing papers of literary criticism is undoubtedly a fine intellectual exercise. But a detailed knowledge of Pope and his contemporaries is not much help in an ordinary classroom, aside from using the rhyming couplet, "Great Anna whom three realms obey / Does sometimes counsel take and sometimes tea," to demonstrate that language is not permanent and fixed. It does change.

I've spent this much time reviewing why the CCCC issued that resolution and what it means because I believe the resolution is important in our attempts to promote literacy. The issue raised in it is not dead. The back-to-basics furor, with a lot of simple-minded notions of what the basics are, and the minimum competency stampede, which stands a good chance of making language differences even more divisive, have increased the importance of the statement.

Finally, after five years, the educational philosophy behind the statement has received some legal recognition. In the summer of 1979 a civil action suit in a United States District Court in Michigan, filed by the parents of fifteen black children who couldn't read very well, was decided in favor of the plaintiffs. The decision was based on the statute that reads: "No State shall deny equal educational opportunity to an individual on account of his or her race, color, sex, or national origin by . . . the failure by an educational agency to take appropriate action to overcome language barriers that impede equal participation by its students in its instructional programs." After listening to the children, their mothers, the teachers and school officials, and a number of linguistic experts, the judge found that the defendant school board had not "taken steps (1) to help the teachers understand the problem; (2) to help provide them with knowledge about the children's use of a 'black English' language system; and (3) to suggest ways and means of using that knowledge in teaching the students to read." He ordered the school board to submit within thirty days a proposal of appropriate action and said that "since the language barrier was found to be a barrier *on the part of the teachers* [my emphasis] . . . the plan should be directed at assisting the teacher."

On August 24, 1979, the judge approved the proposed plan. The professional staff of the Martin Luther King, Junior, Elementary School was to be paid for attending at least twenty hours of an in-service workshop in which three of the eleven objectives were to help the teachers "be able to describe in general the concept of a dialect and dialect differences within the English language"; "be sensitive to the value judgments about dialect differences which people often make and communicate to others"; and "use miscue analysis to distinguish between a dialect shift and a decoding mistake when analyzing an oral reading sample."

The whole of Judge Joiner's forty-three-page decision seems to me cautiously reasoned and clearly written. It's worth reading in its entirety, but some sections at least should be quoted. In summarizing the expert testimony, the judge commented that "efforts to instruct the children in standard English by teachers who failed to appreciate that the children speak a dialect which is acceptable in the home and peer community can result in the children becoming ashamed of their language, and thus impede the learning process. In this respect, the black dialect appears to be different than the usual foreign languages because a foreign language is not looked down on by the teachers" (p. 16). He said further that

> the research evidence supports the theory that the learning of reading can be hurt by teachers who reject students because of the "mistakes" or "errors" made in oral speech by "black English" speaking children who are learning standard English. This comes about because "black English" is commonly thought of as an inferior method of speech and those who use this system may be thought of as "dumb" or "inferior." The child who comes to school using the "black English" system of communication

and who is taught that this is wrong loses a sense of values
related to mother and close friends and siblings and may rebel at
efforts by . . . teachers to teach reading in a different language.
(p. 18)

In applying the current state of knowledge to the problem at King Elementary School, the judge said:

> The teachers in King School had no difficulty in understanding
> the students or their parents in the school setting and the
> children could understand the teachers and other children in
> that setting. In other words, so far as understanding is con-
> cerned . . . although there was initially a type of language
> difference, there was no barrier to understanding caused by the
> language. . . . If a barrier exists because of the language used
> by the children in this case, it exists not because the teachers
> and students cannot understand each other, but because in the
> process of attempting to teach the students how to speak stan-
> dard English the students are made somehow to feel inferior and
> are thereby turned off from the learning process. (pp. 25–26)

The judge noted the children's skill in oral English and
commented on their ability to shift dialects. He said,
"Their speech in court was highly intelligible and contained only traces of 'black English.' This is true although the court heard tapes played of the same children
in casual conversation in which talking among themselves their speech was a true 'black English' vernacular.
In oral speech, though, they seem to quickly adapt to
standard English in settings where it appears to be the
proper language" (p. 31).

In applying the law, Judge Joiner said that this case
dealt with "one of the most important and pervasive
problems facing modern urban America—the problem of
why 'Johnnie Can't Read' when Johnnie is black and
comes from a scatter low income housing unit, set down

in an upper middle class area of one of America's most liberal and forward-looking cities" (p. 34).

The judge did not find that the teachers or the school officials were deliberately discriminating; instead, he found that they were well-meaning—and ill-informed. They did not understand the distinctions among Francis's Grammar I, Grammar II, and Grammar III; that different dialects operate by different rules; that they were making unjustified assumptions about language and ability based on Grammar III. Judge Joiner is not a linguist, but he was able to follow the arguments of qualified linguists, and he based his ruling on a sound recognition of what language is, how we learn it, how it relates to the ability to read and write, and how it often determines our vision of ourselves and who we are.

The problems we cause by our attitude toward dialect differences are not confined to black children, although this case was concerned solely with them. It's a problem that affects large numbers of children from a wide variety of ethnic backgrounds, including many Caucasians whose great-great-grandparents were born in this country. It affects all children whose home language is noticeably different from the school language. It affects not just elementary children learning to read, but older children and adults, whenever surface differences in their language habits are used to label them "dumb" or "inferior."

That Michigan decision applies to only one school in one school system in one state. (The judge had said that the defendant could, if it chose, present a broader plan, but apparently the Ann Arbor School District Board decided to go no further than the law compelled them to go.) It's not likely that all the children in the King Elementary School will become skillful and discriminating readers. Learning to read is a complicated process, and a language barrier on the teacher's part is only one aspect of the problem. Reading difficulties can come from learning disabilities; from emotional maladjustment; from having no role models who are themselves readers; from lack of interest in the material, either because it's unfamiliar or because it's boring; and from other causes too varied to list, some of which have not yet been identified by the experts. Nevertheless, those children stand a better chance of becoming better readers if their teachers stop making value judgments about their language and about them.

Reading with comprehension means getting an idea out of a writer's head into a reader's head, and that idea is more likely to be lodged without distortion in the head of a reader if it is transformed into the variety of language with which the reader feels comfortable. The girl who can paraphrase "Mike was refused permission to draw out books as the result of an unpaid fine" to "Mike couldn't get no more books 'cause he owed money" has read with comprehension, but she won't get much further in her reading ability if the teacher, instead of praising what Jenny can do, says "You're not reading what's on the page, and it's always wrong to say 'couldn't get no more.' " An older Jenny may have trouble discriminating between sense and nonsense, between distortion and straight news in the evening paper—providing, of course, that she progresses far enough to read the paper—because her attention will be centered on the words themselves rather than on the sense the words make in a larger context. It's pretty certain she won't read for fun; she's been deprived of the excitement that can come from looking at print and discovering meaning.

The Michigan decision concentrated on reading; it said almost nothing about the problems students face in learning to write. Although there is no single standard spoken dialect in America, we come much closer to conformity in the way we write. The CCCC committee called that conformity edited American English—the kind of writing that results when somebody, and very often more than one person, has carefully gone over a first or a third draft to make it more conventional.

The special dialect called edited American English is new to all students when they begin school. Learning to talk comes naturally; we aren't conscious of doing it, but, to borrow Jim Raymond's phrase, "Writing is an unnatural act." On its most elementary level, learning to read involves learning to translate the symbols of print into the symbols of sound; learning to write means reversing the process, and the reversal is a good deal harder to master. When we learn to write, we have to produce the symbols—the letters—ourselves, and the oddities of the English spelling system are a poor fit with all modern English dialects. On a less elementary level, learning to write involves a great deal more than transforming speech into written words. It involves learning to compose, learning to sort and arrange ideas, and to put those ideas into words that will deliver a coherent message to whoever reads what we've written.

Coherent written messages can be produced in any dialect, but beginning writers are discouraged if readers react to the lack of editing instead of the content of the message. Johnny won't get much beyond third-grade writing level, whatever that is, unless his teacher treats his early efforts as real attempts at real communication. Let's suppose that Johnny has written a paragraph asking why he was marked absent when it wasn't his fault that the bus broke down. Let's suppose the teacher's only response has been, "You've misspelled *when;* it has an *h* in it. If you ask a question, you must use a question mark. And 'Yesterday I try to' is bad English." If the teacher, who understood perfectly well what Johnny wanted to know, had explained the attendance system and sympathized a bit over Johnny's bad luck, Johnny might have discovered that writing can be a useful tool. He discovered, instead, that writing is a game between him and the teacher, a game the teacher always wins. Johnny is not likely to spend time on the conventions of punctuation, paragraphing, capitalization, and spelling. He won't learn the editing that could make his writing easier to read. Next time he really wants an answer, he'll decide that talking is a safer way to get it.

Good writing always has a purpose—to inquire, to inform, to interpret, to persuade, to come to terms with ourselves and our world—and that purpose serves as a guide to what gets written. Good writing is clear and vigorous, not vapid and vague. It may not always have topic sentences at the head of its paragraphs, but it has some kind of organization, some pattern of development, that readers can follow. It never leaves readers wondering how the writer got from here to there. Good writing is specific. It gives the details and examples that readers will need for understanding. Good writing can be, and is, produced by speakers of every American dialect, but it is more likely to be produced by students who aren't frantically concerned about making mistakes.

We'll get a good deal further in producing acceptable writers if we can convince our students, and ourselves, that sound content, not surface conventions, makes the difference between good writing and bad. Compared with content, conventions are relatively unimportant, even trivial. Good writing can be edited to make it conform to what readers expect—most published writing is edited by at least one other person after the writers consider it finished—but no amount of conventional correctness can compensate for shallow, careless thinking.

By the time those Johnnies and Jennies arrived at the community college where I taught, most of them believed that the only things teachers cared about was conventional correctness. They knew language habits were used to divide, and they were resigned to being on the wrong side of the division line. The praise and the *A*'s had both gone to the students who arrived at school talking like the teacher. They weren't sure why they had trouble reading their psychology texts, but they told me sadly that they'd never been any good in English, that they didn't know any grammar.

My first step was demonstrating that they were experts in the essentials of English grammar (Francis's Grammar I), even though they couldn't explain what they knew (Francis's Grammar II), and my second step was convincing them that I cared more about what they had to say than about how they said it (Francis's Grammar III). The demonstration I used was very simple. I gave them eight words arranged in alphabetical order—a, badly, cafeteria, needs, new, school, this, very—and asked them to rearrange the words so that they made sense. Everybody in the class could do it. Some of them said, "This school very badly needs a new cafeteria"; and others said, "This new school needs a cafeteria very badly"; but nobody produced nonsense, such as "This badly needs a new cafeteria school very." Then we talked about how they came up with those sensible arrangements. They didn't know, of course; all they could say was, "It sounded right." After a lot of discussion, however, they were ready to agree that "knowing what makes sense" is the equivalent of "knowing the essentials of English grammar," even though there are often minor variations in the way we make that sense. Then we went on from there, concentrating first on the meaning of what they wrote, its organization, logic, and clarity, and then on the etiquette of how they wrote it. Their papers needed editing—a lot of editing—but they helped each other with that, and they were surprised to discover that they'd picked up a lot of conventional usage they could apply when they thought it was worth it.

After I'd told them what I know about dialects, about how people learn language, and about what I consider important in talking and writing, I went on to remind them about the language prejudices they could expect to find in employers, acquaintances, and other teachers. Understanding that a lot of what passes for right and wrong in writing is half ignorance and half elitism freed them to make faster progress with their own language abilities. It's only fair to be honest about how people react to language differences, and I didn't want them running down to the schools their own children attend and attacking the teachers, as a couple of them threatened to do.

All of us—teachers, students, concerned citizens, school boards, the Exxon Company, and American Tel and Tel—want the same thing. We want all students to achieve the highest degree of literacy of which they are capable. The disagreement comes in how to go about it. The back-to-basics people think it can be done by starting with spelling and rules, commas and rules, memorizing a list of prepositions, making pronouns agree, and wiping out dialect distinctions—all things that are easy to test. Some of the rest of us think such approaches are too superficial, that real literacy for everybody begins with helping students learn to reason, to see the world they live in honestly and clearly, to communicate in whatever dialect they grew up speaking.

When all students learn to respect themselves and their own language, then we can help them edit their writing. As we work on the editing, however, we need to remember a few very important things.

The first is that changing long-established language habits is never easy. Teachers will need patience; the change will be slow. And the effects of trying to change can seem disastrous. Speech gets muddled, writing gets tangled, and language users seem to be moving backward at a faster rate than they ever went forward. When we fret too much about how we're saying it, we lose track of what it is. When we worry too much about how we're writing, while we're writing, the what gets lost.

In the last two or three years I've seen a striking example of how difficult even a little change can be, not for the students whose habits we're trying to alter, but for ourselves, the professionals who often act as if saying, "Here's the rule, just follow it," would be enough. Because I'm a member of NCTE's women's committee, I was asked to analyze a year's issue of a professional journal to see whether it was using sexist language. The journal carries the statement that contributors are asked to comply with NCTE's *Guidelines for Non-sexist Use of Language,* and the editor tries, I know, to respect the sensibilities of the committed women who read the journal. Yet over and over again in these articles, writers of goodwill talk about *the* teacher and what *he* should do for *his* students. Then they remember to write, "When the student turns in his or her paper. . . ." A paragraph later they've forgotten and say, "The student can use *his* errors. . . ." These writers know the rule, and they're trying. We could—and some people do—use these little slips from recommended usage as a way of dividing the writers into "good guys" and "bad guys," but that would be both unfair and imprecise, unfair because the writers *were* trying, and imprecise because half of them were female. I'm certainly not criticizing the editor, whom I respect and admire. To reject these contributions to the theory of composition teaching would be a sad loss, just as it's a sad loss to reject the sound arguments students have written merely because, in their attempts at editing, they slipped over some of these deeply ingrained habits.

I don't have much trouble with the sexist *he,* partly because I never had much to do with *the* student, but only with a group of individual students, and I never knew *the* teacher, only a lot of individual teachers trying in a lot of contradictory ways to help their students become literate. Nevertheless, like everybody else, I have some language habits that are hard to break. When a voice on the telephone says, "May I speak to Liz McPherson, please," four out of five times I catch myself saying, "This is she." I don't want to. The *she* sounds stilted and pedantic, and when language-users are divided into the stuffy and the natural-sounding, I don't want to land on the stuffy side. Even so, it's only now and then that I can remember to say, "Speaking."

Another important thing to keep in mind is that some language habits are so unimportant they aren't worth the bother. It's only now and then that a member of my family, one who thinks we ought to be language snobs even if we aren't, remembers to tell the dog to *lie* down. I'm glad to report that the dog responds equally well, or more often doesn't respond at all, to either *lie* or *lay.* In fact, the dog, who seems to have a better grasp of language realities than a lot of teachers, is more likely to flop on the rug when she hears, "Lay down," because the lay-down speaker is more reliable about filling the food bowl. It's clear to the puppy that you can't judge the value or the reliability of a human being by the language choices that person makes.

People, more sophisticated than animals, have always made such judgments. In this country, however, there used to be a strong faith that universal education could do a lot to destroy these differences between people. Nowadays, I think, very few people believe that literacy can make everybody equal, that learning to read and write can make everybody healthy, wealthy, and wise, that everybody can rise to the top and nobody will remain at the bottom. Instead, we're left with the rather uninspiring notion that unless you can read and write competently, you won't get a job in the shoe factory—and even if you can, maybe you won't.

With the disappearance of the faith that if you just got educated you could get anywhere has come dissatisfaction with what the schools are doing. A lot of people are accusing the schools of not keeping the promise they thought was being made. Actually, the promise has been pretty well kept. The U.S. Bureau of the Census says the illiteracy rate in this country now is less than 1 percent, roughly the percentage of the population with severe visual or mental impairment. Claims that the rates are higher and still climbing rest on tests or surveys where the cut-off scores have been arbitrarily set. The test-makers and the survey-takers are defining literacy according to their own notions rather than on the basis of common sense. It's become fashionable for the press to bemoan the supposed fact that literacy is declining, that students know less than they used to know, that the public school system is failing. And that's too bad.

We've got a public relations job ahead of us. It would be useful for people to know that language and how it's learned can be, and have been, studied scientifically. A great deal of respectable research has gone on in the last few years, research that could be applied by teachers just as doctors apply the research in medicine or the Pentagon applies the research in destructive weapons. People shouldn't have to go to court, as those Michigan mothers did, to force the schools into using that new knowledge. Nobody wants doctors to treat their ailments by the methods used a hundred years ago, but people still expect the schools to use the drills and diagraming used when they went to school. Everybody seems to know more than the experts about how language should be taught.

As Vivian Davis said some years ago, "If we believe that language can transcend the barriers of human separation and unite us, then we ought to use it to bring ourselves and them 'out there' closer together." We need to get a more realistic picture of why "they" are disappointed, and they need to get a more realistic picture of what we're trying to do.

We need some PR work among ourselves, too. We need to remind the purists among us that the English language is not being damaged, isn't even being dented, by the way its speakers use it. As long as America stays powerful, American English will stay living and strong. In spite of the oil cartel, we're not likely to find ourselves speaking Arabic, although a few new words may arrive to enrich the language. All of us can stop trying to give American English the protection it doesn't need, and, using all the new knowledge that's available to us, turn our efforts to our proper business—making sure that all children and adults can read with discrimination and write with honesty.

Universal literacy can't wipe out poverty and unemployment—the causes are too complex for that—but the more genuine literacy we can achieve, for the greater number of people, the better chance we stand of doing even that. If we'd stop using language differences to divide us, and begin using language similarities to unite us, we'd get more real literacy in this country.

Ridgefield, Washington

Bibliography

Davis, Vivian. "Our Excellence: Where Do We Grow From Here?" *College Composition and Communication* 30 (February 1979): 26.

Francis, W. Nelson. "Revolution in Grammar." *Quarterly Journal of Speech* 40 (October 1954): 299–312.

Martin Luther King, Junior, Elementary School Children et al. v. *Ann Arbor School District Board.* 473 F. Supp. 1371, D.Ct. Mich., 1979.

Silver, Roy S. "High Court Appeal Likely on Book Ban." *New York Times,* August 5, 1979, sec. 1, p. 17.

"Students' Right to Their Own Language." *College Composition and Communication* 25 (Fall 1974).

Whipp, Leslie T. "Teaching English and Social-Class Relationships." *College Composition and Communication* 30 (May 1979): 141–45.

Litəracy
part two

Testing: Art or Illusion?

How Competent Are the Writing Competency Tests?

THOMAS NEWKIRK

Competency examinations are often so thickly shrouded with jargon about validity, reliability, and standard deviations that they seem invulnerable to critical inquiry by ordinary teachers and parents. In this article, Thomas Newkirk, an assistant professor at the University of New Hampshire, removes the mystery—and part of the credibility—by examining a number of writing exercises required on some of the more celebrated exams.

When I taught English at Boston Trade High School, I dreaded days when I had to administer standardized tests. Normally cheerful students would become sullen, and normally sullen students would become belligerent. But one day, due to one test, I almost had a real insurrection on my hands.

The test day was a winter Monday. The building temperature was edging toward 60°. There was broken glass on the floor of my homeroom, the result of weekend vandalism. I handed out the tests, and my welders and cabinetmakers reluctantly went to work. I glanced through the test and immediately spotted trouble. Half way through, the students would have to explicate a poem that, it would seem, had been written by someone from the Hallmark Card Company. "Go lovely O Rose" it began.

As I expected, when the leader of the welders reached "Go lovely O Rose" he slammed his number two pencil down and said "I quit." Whereupon the rest of the welders did the same thing, whereupon the cabinetmakers slammed their pencils down and also stopped work. I made a halfhearted attempt to explain why they should go on—something about the invaluable diagnostic information the test would provide—but there was no response. Finally I did the only thing I could think of: I made it a group project and I helped.

I'm not sure if what I did was a crime. If so the statute of limitations has expired and I can confess. At the very least I fouled up some statistics. But what I retain from that Monday is not guilt but anger, anger that such an inappropriate test could be chosen for my students. It has also caused me to look with a skeptical eye at standardized tests; so if the following examination of writing tests may seem unduly negative, it is because I see unfair testing as a form of child abuse.

Put yourself in the place of a student. You are to take a competency test that is to determine whether you repeat eighth grade. You joke with your friends before the bell, but you're scared. You walk into the classroom and are handed the test, the first part of which asks you to write a report. The teacher reads the instructions:

> In the box below are some facts about the moon which you can use in your report. You may add other facts that you can remember about the moon from your reading and classwork, from television, and from listening to people. . . .
> Be sure to report the facts in an order that will make sense to your classmates.
> Facts about the Moon:
Made of rock

> Mountainous, contains craters
> Covered with dust
> No air or water
> No plant or animal life[1]

You stare at the list and try to remember what you know about the moon. Never did like astronomy anyway. Some words flit through your head—Apollo, lunar, Armstrong—but you can't seem to fit them into a pattern. You connect the facts into three choppy sentences and stop. Well, you think, I do have some friends in seventh grade.

I submit that this is not a farfetched possibility. The "writing" test is not fabricated by me, but is one developed by the National Assessment of Educational Progress (NAEP), and, if the present trend continues, it will find its way into some state competency test of writing. Students, given no opportunity to choose their subjects or gather information, will be evaluated on their ability to write reports.

I have recently examined a number of writing tests that are being constructed or used by states. To my mind most are seriously deficient. I find equally disturbing the reluctance of individual states and local districts to develop their own tests and the reliance they place on the NAEP or on private testmakers such as the Educational Testing Service. A hidden curriculum is being developed by independent and semi-independent organizations. Not only is it a hidden curriculum, but it is one that reflects some of the worst current practices in the teaching of writing—triviality, inadequate time allotment, a confused notion of "creative writing," and the poor choice of writing topics.

Triviality. According to Gary Hart, author of the California Pupil Proficiency Bill, one of the purposes of competency testing is to restore meaning to the high school diploma and thus improve the public's attitude toward its schools.[2] This rationale is echoed by most proponents of competency testing. Yet many of the tests devised are either so simple or so marginal to the basic skills of writing that they would hardly meet Mr. Hart's objective.

Tennessee, for example, will assess competence in spelling and grammar, but not in writing. On one of the items devised for an early version of New York State Competency Tests, students were asked to use "will eat" in a sentence. According to the rules for scoring, all students must do is to write the sentence with no mechanical errors. So presumably, "I will eat" would receive full credit.[3]

One of the proficiency tests that is generally taken as a model was developed by the Denver, Colorado, school system. Students have to do no writing on these exams, but are given what is called a "Language Proficiency Exam" that requires the student to proofread fifty lines that "might have been written by a student."[4] "Language Proficiency" becomes synonymous with "proofreading." Another proficiency test, proclaimed by its developers as a success, is used in the Westlake, Nebraska school system. The writing section requires the student to write three related paragraphs, containing no more than five grammatical errors, on a topic agreed to by the teacher.[5]

Such attempts at measuring writing competency are inadequate, not because the mechanics of writing are unimportant, but because "proficient" writing is more than "correct" writing. Imagine the student navigating his way through the three required paragraphs at Westlake, aware that his primary task is to avoid errors. He may avoid syntactic errors by using short sentences; he avoids spelling errors by using simple words or circumlocutions; he avoids contractions, and, in general, tries to be as timid and safe as possible.

Such tests reinforce the negative image many Americans have about writing. Donald Graves has described this attitude: "In America, writing is basically a form of etiquette in which words are put on paper, not necessarily with clarity, but free of mechanical errors. The American does not belong in writing. He is similar to the person who has been reluctantly invited to a party of distinguished guests. Being a person of modest station he attends with great discomfort. He has but one thing on his mind—to be properly attired, demonstrate the finest manners, say nothing, and leave quickly."[6]

Inadequate Time Allotment. Most of the tests that do require student writing limit the time allowed. The Educational Testing Service, for example, is currently marketing a test of basic skills that includes in the writing section a number of multiple-choice questions and a twenty-minute writing sample on an assigned topic. In its manual for the test, the ETS claims that its exercises were developed "after a comprehensive review of the [relevant] research" and after consultation with professional organizations.[7]

The research that supports such a test was primarily conducted by the ETS itself; the most thorough study was reported by Godshalk, Swineford, and Coffman in 1966. In essence, the researchers gave a large group of students impromptu essay tests on assigned topics and used the average score as the base against which they measured the effectiveness of their hour-long composition test. This test consisted of a number of multiple-choice questions on sentence structure, some editing exercises, and a twenty-minute essay on an assigned topic. They found that there was a high correlation between the average score on the four essays and the scores on the hour-long test.[8]

Yet despite the sophistication and scope of the Godshalk study, it fails to demonstrate the validity of the timed impromptu essay as a measure of writing competence. The researchers took as their definitive measure of writing ability the scores on four impromptu essays. Never did the researchers look at writing done under looser time constraints where the student had some choice of topic. The Godshalk study does not prove the validity of impromptu essay tests; it assumes their validity.

Recent research has raised questions about the use of the impromptu essay. Sanders and Littlefield found that the impromptu essay can fail to reveal the skills students have mastered, particularly if a course emphasizes the writing process—prewriting, revising, editing. They unequivocally reject the use of the impromptu essay as a measure of writing competence: "The rigidly controlled essay test surely represents the ultimate in an artificial writing situation; as such it is shunned in many modern composition courses. While the test essay is precisely timed, in many courses the student is encouraged to think, research, write, rewrite, perhaps solicit advice and reactions, and rewrite again and again. The student has no chance to go through this process in writing an impromptu essay."[9]

The twenty-minute essay also sends a curious educational message. Research on the composing processes of good and poor secondary-school or college-freshmen writers is beginning to reveal consistent differences.[10] The poorer writer generally spends little time prewriting, writes in a burst, and then spends no time revising. Better writers spend far more time planning and pausing to reread what they have written. It is this time spent contemplating and planning that distinguishes the good from the poor writers. So what does the twenty-minute essay do? It forces the good writers to modify their composing processes to resemble those of poor writers. Good writing habits must be discarded. Competency tests, then, require the more competent to imitate the less competent.

As for the claim that the ETS has consulted national organizations, this seems unlikely in the case of the writing section. But then "consultation" can mean many things. The most respected guide for the conduct of research, the NCTE monograph *Research in Written Composition,* argues that "twenty to thirty minutes seems ridiculously brief for a high school or college student to write anything thoughtful." The authors recommend that high school students be given seventy to ninety minutes to write.[11] John Mellon, a researcher assigned by the NCTE to evaluate the NAEP results, claims that a fair sample of a student's work would consist of 800 to 1000 words drawn from four or five essays.[12]

At its root the issue is ethical and not purely experimental. And the ethical question is simple. If states are to assess the writing competence of students, are they not under the ethical obligation to allow them to write under the best possible conditions? If so, is not one of these conditions adequate time to plan, write, and revise?

Creative Writing. One of the early criticisms of the NAEP exercises was their functional orientation. Unfortunately, the exercises developed to meet this objection illustrate the current confusion about "creative writing." Too often creative writing translates into fictional writing, where students must imagine themselves in situations far removed from their own experiences. Creativity becomes fantasizing, and frequently these fantastical creations are curiously impersonal, stereotypical imitations of the fantasies students watch on TV. Another type of creative writing exercise is to ask students to "write what they feel," an exercise in formlessness. Both types of writing are called for on some state tests.

The following exercise, developed by the NAEP, was adopted by the Ohio Department of Education for its eighth grade writing test. The purpose of the exercise, according to the Ohio manual, was for the student to "demonstrate ability in writing to reveal personal feelings and ideas through free expression." Here is the assignment:

> Sometimes people write just for the fun of it. This is a chance for you to have fun writing. Pretend you are a pair of tennis shoes. You've done all kinds of things in all kinds of weather. Now you are picked up again by your owner. Tell what you, as a pair of tennis shoes, think about what is going to happen to you. Tell how you feel about your owner.[13]

Surely there are better ways to assess personal writing than this. To my mind, the most convincing expression of personal feeling came from a student who wrote, "I don't know." The response was classified as "other."

In another NAEP exercise students were shown a picture of five children playing on an overturned dory. The dory is on a dock that reaches out to a small inlet where sailboats are moored. The instructions were:

> These kids are having fun jumping on the overturned boat. Imagine you are one of the children in the picture. Or if you wish, imagine you are someone standing nearby watching the children. Tell what is going on as he or she would tell it. Write as if you are telling this to a good friend, in a way that expresses strong feelings. Help your friend feel the experience too.[14]

Such an exercise violates the most basic rules for writing assignments. In the first place, the children in the picture seem to be about eight years old, and few adolescents of thirteen or seventeen (the age of those given the test by the NAEP) would enjoy writing about children so much younger than they are. And although I distrust the automatic criticism of socioeconomic bias, it does seem likely that the setting would be unfamiliar to students who have spent no time at seaside or lakeside resorts.

But the biggest problem with the assignment is that it invites a sophisticated phoniness. The following piece written by a seventeen-year-old was given a top rating by the NAEP judges, who determined that it demonstrates an "imaginative entry into experience":

> Jumping and running on the boat's very enjoyable. Up we jump and down we float. I feel as if I could sail the boat around the world and back. The salty air blows through my nostrils. My body is engulfed in this salty concoction. The wind beats against my cheeks.
>
> The white glistening enamel underside of the boat feels like silk (?) to the touch. The trees are alive, pulsating, watching our childish games.
>
> I feel like I could play forever. No concept of time, no stresses encourage my exhuberance.
>
> My body separated from my spirit. I am no longer encaged in a prison of bones and skin. There are no barriers now. I can do whatever I want, whenever I want.[15]

I sensed a skilled writer performing an awkward task. The writer has been pushed into a difficult and, I believe, dishonest stance by a topic that on one hand asks for strong personal writing and on the other takes the writer away from what he or she feels strongly about.

Finally, some exercises give so little guidance that it is difficult to see how the writing could be evaluated. Wash-

ington state has used the following exercise in its eighth
grade writing test:

> Music does different things to different people. Perhaps it makes
> you feel one way or another. Perhaps it reminds you of some place
> or something happening. Now listen to this piece of music and
> write what things this piece of music does to you. Start writing
> any time you wish.[16]

Would a student taking this test have any idea of what is
expected?

Poor Topics.   Writing must be about something. It is not
some set of disembodied skills that can be assessed apart
from the act of communication about a subject. *The greatest and most consistent weakness of the NAEP writing
exercises is their failure to ask students to write on subjects they know something about.* The exercises move the
students into areas where their knowledge is severely
limited. They often find themselves in some hypothetical
territory where they must be "creative," or they are pushed
into what Donald Graves has called "extended territory,"
writing about national and international events and personalities. When students must write about this extended territory, without a chance to do research, they
often write with limited information. A typical exercise:

> Everyone knows of something that is worth talking about. May-
> be you know something about a famous building like the Empire
> State Building in New York City or something like the Golden
> Gate Bridge in San Francisco. Or you might know a lot about the
> Mormon Tabernacle in Salt Lake City or the new sports sta-
> diums in Atlanta or St. Louis. Or you may be familiar with
> something from nature like Niagara Falls, a gigantic wheat
> field, a grove of orange trees, or a part of a wide muddy river like
> the Mississippi. Choose something you know about. It may be
> something you have seen while traveling or something you have

studied in school. Think about it for a while and then write a description of what it looks like so that it could be recognized by someone who read your description.[17]

While ostensibly this is an open assignment, the implication is that the student should write about something "important," something well known, and not something as insignificant as the student's home or school or favorite park. The writing that such exercises elicit invariably deals with extended territory and illustrates the difficulty students have. The following piece was written for a similar NAEP assignment, which required students to write on a person they admired. As might be expected, the possibilities suggested were all male national or international figures—Mickey Mantle, Winston Churchill, Martin Luther King, Jr. The following piece was rated in the eighty-seventh percentile of the work done by seventeen-year-olds:

> Dr. Christian Bernard: I believe he is a person worth looking up to. He has tried to make our life longer for us through research about operations on heart transplants. His determination to help mankind is recognized even though public opinion is very much against the practice of transferring one person's heart to another person. This determination shows how a true doctor or any kind of scientist would work for the betterment of mankind, both for a longer life and an easier world to live in. Dr. Bernard shows the dedication of a true doctor, to help man when he is sick or dying, as are many of the people on whom he operates. His determination makes him try to show the world that the heart is not a sacred organ of the body, and is just like any other part of the body when it needs to be repaired. His determination to find a better method, new drugs to help after surgery is to be admired. This is one of the reasons I admire him.[18]

I find this writing dismal, what Ken Macrorie has called "Engfish." The student has nothing specific to say about Dr. Bernard and must resort to abstractions and platitudes. But again the writer was pushed into this position by the assignment.

The most confusing NAEP topic asks the student to write a letter of application. The exercise shows a notice of a job opening in a clothing store and gives the following directions:

> Chris Jones lives at 3600 Larch Street in New York, New York 10004. Chris has finished the junior year at high school and has been looking for a summer job. Chris spotted the advertisement in the *New York Times* and decided to apply for the job. Write Chris' letter to Mr. Fried.[19]

The student is again put in a curious position. He is to write Chris's letter although he knows nothing about Chris except his address and year in school. What is even more puzzling is the NAEP's method for evaluating the letter. To be awarded the higher marks the letter must include references, a statement of qualifications, and a way to be contacted. While these are valid criteria for a letter of application, the instructions do not make clear the necessity of the student's inventing such information.

The fact that most states are looking for minimal competencies does not lessen the need for good topics. When a student must write without information, not only does content suffer, but everything else suffers. Students cannot develop a paragraph if they have nothing to put into it. Students will have trouble with transitions if they have no information to transit from and to. They will have trouble maintaining a thesis on a topic they care little about. Unfortunately, the NAEP topics have failed to motivate extensive writing. In the second-round writing assessment, for example, the average length of writing for seventeen-year-olds was 137 words, with a sizable minority writing only one paragraph.[20] I would question any conclusions, even on writing mechanics, that might be drawn from such obviously unmotivated writing.

Motivation will become an increasingly serious problem if states and local districts move toward the primary trait scoring system developed in connection with the NAEP exercises. Briefly, primary trait scoring is an alternative to holistic scoring, where general qualities such as organization, ideas, and style are evaluated in different types of writing. Rather, it is argued that each type of writing has specific traits and therefore the criteria for evaluation should change as the writing task changes. Primary trait scoring, then, is more than a system of evaluation; it involves the construction of writing tasks in such a narrow way that specific skills or primary traits can be evaluated.

In practice, though, there are two problems with this system of writing assignments. The first has to do with the way "purpose" comes to be used. One text that promotes such assignments states:

> You will see that each [exercise] is carefully designed *to present students with a purpose* and to challenge them to develop appropriate means to achieve that purpose [my emphasis].[21]

The term *purpose* according to my dictionary means "fixed determination." I can see how a teacher can foster such determination, can encourage it, or can create situations in which the students actually feel it. But we can no more present the students with purposes than we can present them with happiness. There is something coldly external about the way the term is used. Aims "presented" from the outside in this way, especially when combined with assigned audiences who won't really read the pieces ("Imagine you were to write to your congressman . . . "), can only encourage phony gameplaying.

A second and related problem has to do with narrowness. The assignments can easily become so specific that the student has no experience or information to draw on. A sense of ownership is lost. One article advocating an assignment system similar to the primary trait system contrasts an "unsatisfactory" assignment with a "more satisfactory one."

> Unsatisfactory assignment:
>   Write a statement of your beliefs about some subject important to you.
> More satisfactory assignment:
>   You find yourself the apparent leader of _____ Club. You and your members have agreed to formalize your organization's constitution. The preamble should state your feelings and beliefs clearly and forcefully. You might want to read the preambles to several constitutions in order to better prepare for writing your own.[22]

I will make no defense of the first assignment except to say that I prefer it over the second. The second, though more specific, leaves the student no room to maneuver. Assigned an aim, a role, an organizational pattern, the student can only follow directions.

Any writing competency test must begin with a definition. What is writing? I would argue that the tightly specific exercises that the NAEP is using do not test writing because the assignments themselves make decisions that the writer should make. Decisions about purpose, content, point of view, focus, and language are at the heart of the writing process—they are the writing process. Assignments that present the student with a subject, with a role, with information, with an organization, are calling for a lobotomized activity.

I use the term *lobotomized* in a literal sense. The great Russian psychologist Alexander Luria studied many cases of frontal brain damage and has observed that a person so injured loses the capacity to form lasting intentions, to plan for the future, or determine a course of behavior.[23] Nevertheless, when presented with a delimited task such as a standard test of intelligence, the patient can perform quite well on it. Is it not possible that we are defining writing competency in such a way that someone with frontal brain damage might be proclaimed competent? Is it not possible that such delimited exercises do not measure that capacity which, according to Luria, makes us truly human, the capacity to form and carry out intentions? And is not this intentionality at the heart of what we call the writing process?

Richard Lloyd-Jones, a proponent of primary trait scoring, acknowledges that narrowly defined writing tasks may fail to motivate students, but he offers no solutions. "The more one restricts the situation in order to define a purpose and stimulate performance of a particular kind, the greater the chances that the exercise will fall outside of the respondents' experiences. The testmaker must deal with the problem directly."[24] Testmakers face conflicting pressures. They must develop a test that truly tests writing—a valid test. And they must develop a test that will be evaluated consistently by raters—a reliable test. As I see it these goals cannot be reconciled; they can only be balanced. Primary trait scoring creates an imbalance with its preoccupation with reliability. Unless a student is motivated to produce his best work, of what value is a precise evaluation instrument? Is precise evaluation so important that students should be given no choice in topics? The British, for example, in writing tests given to students not going on to college, may give as many as ten options, sacrificing some reliability on the chance that the student will find a topic that works. A balance must be struck, and the nature of this balance is a matter of human judgment and not some immutable psychometric law.

Those who promote competency testing must come to realize that they cannot rely on traditional means of assessment. By demanding a measure of *individual* writing competence, they are asking for something that the blunderbuss of mass testing cannot deliver. No single piece of writing can be a measure of writing ability; no single topic can be fair to every student. An alternative to the type of mass testing I've criticized is a folder system, where a student is evaluated on writing done for class. This option is used in a number of British secondary schools. Typically, each student must complete a folder of work, approximately sixteen pieces of writing, during the year in which he or she is being examined. Half of these pieces are transactional (persuasive, informative) and the other half can be poetry, fiction, or personal narratives. Teachers using this system meet regularly to share assignments and to standardize grading. At the end of the year each teacher evaluates the twelve best pieces of work and that evaluation is checked by a second reader, usually a teacher in another school. A third reader may then resolve major discrepancies.

During a fellowship year, I visited a number of British secondary schools that were using folder assessment. Not only did the system seem fairer but it also stimulated good teaching. Students wrote regularly. Teachers could choose topics appropriate to student interests and related to other classwork. *Teachers developed their own writing programs.* By contrast, those teachers who prepared students for traditional certification exams (essay tests constructed and graded by outside examiners) spent most of their time pulling out old exams and putting students through dry runs. Students would write not for the teacher, or their peers, least of all for themselves. They would write for Them, the unknowable but all-powerful examiners. Writing became a way of passing tests.

One morning, not long ago, I set out to read a set of NAEP exercises. The more I read, the more depressed I became. There seemed to be something limiting in setting any task and then devising specific criteria that would apply to all the writing produced. I began to feel like I was in an airless room.

I would wander to the kitchen to fix coffee and listen to my nine-month-old daughter make *b* sounds—"bbbbbB-BBBB," increasing her volume and her smile. I came back to my study, to minimal competencies and primary-trait scoring, reluctantly. I began to read some student work and came to a piece that dispelled the gloom, not because it was superbly written, but because there was in it a sense of delight and humor that made it stand out like a flower pushing through a sidewalk crack. It was written in response to one of the more interesting NAEP topics:

> Imagine you are taking care of a neighbor's children for an afternoon. You send one of the children to the corner store to buy some peaches for a snack. The store owner, Mr. Jones, whom you have known and liked for several years, apparently took advantage of the child. The peaches are rotten. You want to send the child back with the peaches and a note to clear up the situation. Write a note to the grocer that expresses your displeasure and proposes what Mr. Jones should do about the situation.[25]

After exercises requiring the writing of phone messages and letters of request, here we finally had something—melodrama. The following piece clearly baffled the evaluators, who classified it as "generally factual" and "not personally abusive." I like to think of the writer as someone who, as an infant, delighted in making sounds:

Dear Mr. Jones:

I am writing you in regard to the peaches that were purchased by a child I was keeping. I wanted some peaches for a snack but as I bit into one I found to my horror and disgust that they were rotten. Fortunately I kept cool. I tried so hard to forgive and forget, but the child I was keeping obviously couldn't. After eating 12 of your rotten peaches she regurgitated all over the carpet but I tried to endure it because I had a brainstorm. I could feed the remaining peaches to the dog. But as luck would have it upon eating the peaches the dog's hair fell out. However, Mr. Jones, even though these terrible things happened to me I am not mad. I am merely writing to tell you I realized something about you and extend you all my sympathy. Because after this event I now realize why you have no teeth or hair, because you've eaten your own rotten peaches.

Your friend,
Lee Smith

The University of New Hampshire

Notes

1. "Writing: Released Exercises from the 1973–74 Assessment," #203008-NT, National Assessment of Education Progress (Denver, 1976), pp. 180–181.

2. Gary Hart, "The California Pupil Proficiency Law as Viewed by Its Author," *Phi Delta Kappan* 59 (May 1978): 592–95.

3. "The New York State Basic Competency Testing Program: A Brief Overview," The New York State Bureau of Pupil Testing and Advisory Services (1977), p. 9. The New York written exam has changed considerably since 1977 and, in its current form, is one of the best in the country.

4. Donald Henderson, "Denver, Colorado: A 17-Year-Old Minimum Competency Testing Program," *Phi Delta Kappan* 59 (May 1978): 610–11.

5. Jim Findley, "Westlake's Minimum Competency Graduation Requirements: A Program That Works," *Phi Delta Kappan* 59 (May 1978): 614–18.

6. Donald Graves, "Balance the Basics: Let Them Write," An Information Paper for the Ford Foundation (1977), pp. 10–11.

7. *Basic Skills Assessment Technical Manual* (Princeton: Educational Testing Service, 1977), pp. 38 39.

8. Fred I. Godshalk, Frances Swineford, and William Coffman, *The Measurement of Writing Abilities* (New York: College Entrance Examination Board, 1966).

9. Sara Sanders and John Littlefield, "Perhaps Test Essays Can Reflect Significant Improvement in Freshman English," *Research in the Teaching of English* 9 (Fall 1975): 147.

10. Charles Stallard, "An Analysis of the Writing Behavior of Good Writers," *Research in the Teaching of English* 8 (Fall 1974): 206–18.

11. Richard Braddock, Richard Lloyd-Jones, and Lowell Schoer, *Research in Written Composition* (Urbana, Illinois: National Council of Teachers of English, 1963), p. 9.

12. John Mellon, "Round Two of the National Writing Assessment: Interpreting the Apparent Decline in Writing Ability," *Research in the Teaching of English* 10 (Spring 1976): 67.

13. NAEP Released Exercise #101013-N, p. 23.

14. Ibid., p. 33.

15. National Assessment of Educational Progress, *Expressive Writing: Selected Results from the Second National Assessment of Writing* (Denver: ERIC Document Reproduction Service, ED 130–312).

16. "Mathematics/Writing," Washington Statewide Educational Assessment, Eighth Grade Test administered in the fall of 1976.

17. NAEP Released Exercise #R 203012-NT, p. 197.

18. "Group Results A, Science and Writing; Report 5 of the 1969–1970 Assessment," National Assessment of Educational Progress (Denver, 1971), p. B-46.

19. NAEP Released Exercise #203008-NT, pp. 1080–81.

20. Mellon, "Round Two of the National Writing Assessment," p. 67.

21. Carl Klaus et al., *Composing Childhood Experience*, experimental version (St. Louis: CEMREL, 1979), p 10.

22. Eleanor Hoffman and John Schifsky, "Designing Writing Assignments," *English Journal* 66, no. 9 (December 1977): 41–45.

23. A. L. Luria, *The Man with the Shattered World* (New York: Basic Books, 1972), p. 34.

24. Richard Lloyd-Jones, "Primary Trait Scoring," in *Evaluating Writing*, ed. Charles Cooper and Lee Odell (Urbana: National Council of Teachers of English, 1977), p. 42.

25. NAEP Released Exercise #R 201008-S, p. 89.

Who Am I Unless I Know You? Another View of Competence

RICHARD LLOYD-JONES

Since 1963, when he published an NCTE monograph entitled Research in Written Composition *with Richard Braddock and Lowell Schoer, Richard Lloyd-Jones has been concerned with the problems and possibilities of research in the teaching and evaluation of writing. His more recent publications in this area include an article,* "Primary Trait Scoring," *published in* Evaluating Writing: Describing, Measuring, Judging, *an NCTE monograph edited by Charles Cooper and Lee Odell (1977), and* "The Politics of Research into the Teaching of Composition," *published in the October 1977 issue of* College Composition and Communication.

Professor Lloyd-Jones, who is currently chairing the English Department at the University of Iowa, has been consulted in the development of numerous standardized tests, including the English and literature section of the National Teacher Examination, the test of knowledge of usage developed by the American College Testing Program, and the description of performance in writing developed for the National Assessment of Educational Progress (NAEP). In this article he examines standardized tests from both the humanistic and the scientific perspectives.

Mystery lives in language. Any view of human competence that does not begin with this assumption is more dangerous than useful because it encourages a reductive view of the nature of man. Language permits us to know ourselves and "thou" as well as you and it; it governs the realm of spirit where relations are named and through which one comes to know that which cannot be named. Whenever our enthusiasm for making tests entices us to separate some formal feature of language so that it can be encapsulated in an "item," then we have engaged a "structure," as Buber calls it, but we have not demonstrated a human competence to enter into relationships. Whether we offer multiple choices of verb tense or count the number of examples used to substantiate an assertion, we have in a sense sold our birthright for a mess of pottage. By all means let us honor a good bowl of soup, but let us not define ourselves wholly in terms of "it."

Having begun in such grand terms, perhaps I should take a lower path through some standard rhetorical definitions. Even mysteries can be discussed in part in the plain syle. The functions of language can be named as serving two objectives. The first is to make the world, and the second is to allow one user to relate to another and by that act to make one's self. We can instead divide these functions into explanation, persuasion, and expression, or into logic and communication, expressive and transactional discourse, or even, I suppose, into Bain's four modes, if a function can be made into a mode. In the world of daily utility one might even talk separately of the purposes of progress reports, sales brochures, term papers, letters of sympathy, and the like. These little purposes are a help to teachers on Monday morning. They set up situations for discourse.

There are advantages in thinking grandly about the purposes of language in order to avoid being trivialized by pressures of brute survival, though. Some people may argue that the world exists (at least in the mind of God) and thus cannot be made, but for each person the world needs to be made anew in small pieces so that ordinary mortals can live in it. The almost helpless infant must become strong in many ways if it is to be human, but whether we say that it develops myriad synapses, or learns to control abstractions, or masters a symbol system, we are observing tha this creature finds a language to organize one organism's perceptions into a world of meaning. Quite possibly the personally discovered structures also do exist in the world, but the infant must discover them in the forms permitted by language. We are delighted with the first word and impressed with how soon words are made into whole sentences because we recognize the astonishing multiplication of human power that is taking place. We repeat the words and applaud; we patiently offer alternatives to the child's mislabeling of all males as "papa" or cats as "dogs" and know that the child is growing into our language system and our view of the world. Language is our chief vehicle for exploration, and we share it with those dear to us.

In Babel we know that languages divide us, but we sometimes forget that part of the trouble is that separate languages create separate visions of the world. In hope we speak of the United Nations, but the approximations of translators should not really deceive us, for we know that children born into different language cultures not only acquire different values but organize the world differently. Objects have different emotional coding, and levels of abstraction and classification differ according to the need of a culture. Sometimes we contemplate the problems of misunderstanding, like the stories of the end of the Pacific phase of World War Two, where we are told a mistranslated passage led to the dropping of the Bomb and the entry of the Soviets into that part of the war, but any of us who deal in literary texts are constantly caught up by problems of taking the language of one culture and representing it fairly in another. We are amused to hear that Shakespeare is a German author, and not a French one, but if we are clever, we know he is an alien even to modern Americans, few of whom are really comfortable in Jacobean English. We master the world in language, but it is not the same world mastered by those born to other languages. If we ever master those worlds it is because we have made ourselves into suitable audiences for the original language.

Consider even more what happens when we abandon natural language and talk in mathematics or graphics. In a way numbers are international and timeless by virtue of reduction; we cut away the sensory referents that might confuse our emotions with concrete emblems of value, but the act of cutting out much of what the natural language can and must say also rearranges the world. Natural language represents the blend of naming and valuing that is characteristically human. The abstractions of mathematics denature as much as they denationalize, and modern physical scientists are alienated from colleagues in the humanities until they learn to translate numbers into words; for all of the defensive talk about two cultures, the fault does not really lie with the humanist. Some scientists find such an act of translation a useful check on a theory; others find such "simplifications" offensive to their sense of truth to the mathematical idea. Introducing physical objects toward which we inevitably have feelings contradicts the whole system of abstract symbols, even though it also may serve to correct some wild errors. I sympathize with both sides in the argument, and here I have no need to choose one, although in truth I think we have to live in the world of sensations. I merely want to observe that a command of more than one language—natural or invented—allows one to have the world in more than one way. And that is power. The issue is not so much to correct error as it is to conceive of choices in representing the world according to one's need. The choice of what language to use in itself limits the available answers to questions.

My concern in this paper, however, is not with how language controls knowledge, the external world of sensations, but how it controls people conceived separately from the world of objects. The distinction I'm grasping for is analogous to statements made by women when they object to being treated as sex objects instead of as people. They are not denying sexuality, and perhaps not even their status as objects in a world of sensation, but they are insisting that some quality of human animation is more important in defining their nature than the facts of their physical bodies. I am concerned with how the linguistic relationship between speaker and hearer, writer and reader, defines and transcends both. Language and what it denotes provide the context and the representation of the relationship. The most important competence in using the language is not to be discovered in the anatomy of isolated features but in the holistic view of writing and speaking in context.

The competence I'm talking about is acquired by living actively among people. Like the language itself, social competence is primarily manifested in present oral situations, but it is subject to conscious control in relatively timeless written relationships. In speech it is augmented by gesture and physical presence. In writing, the temporal sequence of speech becomes verbal architecture in a page layout, for a reader can observe a beginning and an ending of a paper simultaneously—or nearly so. At least the eye can move back and forth as it does in examining an object. The shape of a discourse has almost literal meaning. In short, the techniques of social awareness are generally learned in speech and translated into writing, an act which requires additional self-awareness and labor, and thus is reserved for major occasions.

It is helpful to see this process within a general view of education. One view of education defines the human as willfully ignorant, manifesting disobedience by finding wrong answers—or at least by failing to learn or recall right answers. Such a theory requires clearly accepted right answers—genuine doubt is not allowed—but even more it defines the child as an inadequate adult who can literally be whipped into shape. I suppose that at least some of the people in this era who talk of negative reinforcement really share these assumptions. The beast in man, the infantile tantrum throwers who think the world was made to serve them, must learn to submit, and even the developmentalists may admit that there is a stage of growth during which these assumptions about punishment have merit. Avoidance of personal discomfort may influence the behavior of children who cannot yet imagine social good or deferred pleasure.

We might instead adopt the blank tablet or empty jug view of education. Here is clay ready to be shaped or wax to be incised by teachers. Perhaps the vessel can be expanded, like a balloon, but essentially the duty of educators is not to change the nature of the jug—indeed, perhaps they cannot change its nature—but rather to supply knowledge and skills as facts to fill the space. Sherlock Holmes told Watson that the mind is an attic that should not be filled with unessential knowledge because no room will be left for what is important. In this world of blank tablets one discovers facts; creation is an anomaly. I take it that this view of education once dominated our schools and perhaps still dominates our colleges. It is lecture and textbook land; the fact is an end in itself. Such a view permits us to believe that students are readily tested en masse, so it is popular for wrong reasons, but that should not obscure the truth that knowledge is useful. We need facts even though we are not jugs.

Probably the favorite theory of our age is "developmental." The word decorates all sorts of courses titles and sometimes serves as a euphemism for what should have been learned at an earlier time in one's life, but we need not rule it out simply because it is fashionable. I think I hear the same principle enunciated in those Romantic paeans to the imagination in the nineteenth-century paradigms. Lord Kelvin may have thought that science dealt with the measurable, and that things which could not be measured were not science, and perhaps didn't exist, but evolution, genetic theory, and even physics itself were headed in other directions. The establishment of kindergartens, the theories of Piaget, variations on organic and biological metaphors, the developments of hierarchies of values, all suggest that humans not merely acquire knowledge but also are changed, developed, and enlarged by that knowledge into different creatures. We are both what we eat and what we learn. That is what we mean by growth, and we can emblemize it in the differences between modern photographic portraits of children as developing humans and older paintings of children as undersized adults. Indeed, even our efforts to define syntactic maturity can be read in these terms. The more complex the syntax, the more we assume the human bud is turning into a flower.

A developmental theory is useful for a rhetorician in terms we can identify with Dewey. Experience for Dewey is more than the accumulation of events to fill the empty vessel of a life; it is an active engagement with the events.

The exercise of the engagement shapes the mind as work on the muscles develops the body. But exercise is not merely repetition, it is incremental. We can borrow another useful term from mathematics, "successive approximation," or its less sophisticated cousin, "trial and error." By implication, in each experience of a process, mistakes are not willful—they are merely the accidental result of inexperienced aim, or the test-firings in the systematic observation of tracer bullets. The child tries a word; the parent offers a better one. The pupil drafts a paper; the teacher-editor suggests improvements. Some have complained that the teacher is thus always cast in the negative role of correcter and the pupil is always demonstrated as inadequate, and that is partly true. It should apply equally to the parent, but we don't think of parents as negative because the correction is supported by affection. The half truth reveals an implied attitude toward error, a vestige of the notion that error is disobedience, so of course any suggestion for change implies a negative statement about the moral value of the errant person. The mistake is an absolute wrong, not a step in a process of discovery. The other half of the truth is that the correcter is a partner in a search. If one is engaged with the pupil in combining the experience of two people to produce an effective statement, then the correction is a product of mutual interest, of a social bond, and affirms support. "Together *we* will find *your* meaning." This alliance is built on affection, and it may be strained if the teacher faces 120 pupils a day.

More, the product of the common seeking for effective statements is not merely overt abstracted knowledge of a schoolroom type, nor even tacit skill, but an altered capacity to do the task. The metaphor of the *tabula rasa* suggests a fixed size, a limited space on which to record knowledge; the developmental metaphors suggest that exercise and nutrition through practice and experiment enable us to handle additional kinds of knowledge.

It is in this developmental sense that the changes in social maturity must be seen. The infant is totally self-centered. It engages in transactions in order to get service—food and comfort—and it submits to force; but it doesn't imagine the motives of others. Discussions of the preschool child abound with descriptions of how children move from an awareness of outsiders as things to be smiled at, adapted to, and played with to a sense that other sentient creatures should be understood. "How would you like it if Billy did X to you?" Thus we lead children to discover analogs of themselves. Although our purpose is probably to change the immediate behavior of the child toward another person, the effect is to insist on the essential similarity of people and to call attention to the child's self by comparing it with another self.

In seeing the analog, the alter ego, this not-I, children can no longer take themselves for granted. The message is that the world does not cease to exist when you close your eyes at bedtime; Mommy really is there when she hides beyond the towel and then look out, saying "peekaboo." These almost changeless games are part of the process of turning the new human from a solipsist into a lap- or porch-child and then into a citizen of the world. At any stage the process may be delayed or totally inhibited and we may find ourselves with a physical adult who is a moral and social infant.

Our expectations about maturity are modest enough. Those who can extend their social imagination to encompass the family and a few close friends win gold stars as responsible citizens. So far, we have not really demanded great humanitarian gestures of adults; although we praise minor altruists as great benefactors, we prefer to assassinate the genuine moral lawgivers. They develop too far ahead of the crowd, and we can't see ourselves being analogized in them. We are threatened by their power to upset conventions more than we are bothered by childish vandals who write on walls. To be sure, once they are safely dead, one may promise to imitate, like the imitators of Christ, but no one is really expected to measure up to the great social discoverers. We are not able to discover ourselves in such people except as projections of fantasy.

In short, in social development most people prefer to stick to their own neighborhood. If one is obliged to examine the motives and creeds of people who are too far estranged from us, or if we must meet too many strangers, we have to make so many comparisons that we can't keep them straight. A good Athenian might not have imagined so many ways to "know thyself." After all, Sparta really was in the neighborhood, and variant choices in discourse with Spartans were not great. The author of the *Republic* must even have liked Spartans. But one of the chief functions of discourse in an electronic world, in a world with writing, tape, and film, is to enlarge the audience far beyond the variety represented in the Greek world and thus to force more refined definitions of the self. Writing exists in this larger framework of discourse, and premature efforts to judge competence on the basis of mechanical forms are misleading. The form out of context has meaning only in a crude sense.

If we are to know about skill in writing, we need first to judge the competence of the writer in recognizing who the writer and the reader are within any specific situation. The relationship is at stake; apart from the relationship, neither exists in discourse. Lewis Thomas's metaphor of the medusa and the snail is perfect for my emblem. In the gyre that represents their continued existence first one and then the other seems to dominate, to be the survivor, but in truth neither organism can continue to exist without the other. To be sure, their knowledge of one another is truly carnal, and they are not alter egos, but still the identity of one without the other is an illusion. One literally feeds off the other.

These flights of metaphors may obscure the humble reality. Children described by Britton and others first use language to grasp the world in the language used by those who tend them; their talk is designed to validate a view of the world. Gradually the children learn rules for varying the rules so as to express their own perceptions and needs to adults and thus engage them in transactions. Since the adults are willing and often able to make the whole effort at interpretation, children need adapt but little except to explain issues the adults cannot otherwise intuit. The more strangers enter the children's worlds, the more these children need to imagine what listeners actually hear and thus to frame their discourse to fit the needs of these other persons. The shyness of children must surely be in part a reaction to the awareness of such alienation from other creatures, the appreciation that differing wills must be coped with. By the time they are old enough for school, the sense of otherness develops rapidly in face-to-face meetings, although report cards still have places to record additional progress in deportment. And even adults do not fully master these transactions. Consider how many of us who lecture, even though we are worldly, have trouble deciding whether what we frame so artfully is even understood by our audience. We won't ask whether some of our best classes for the students are those which are messy, with loose ends, and offensive to our sense of art.

By the time children have become basically social they can focus on the bare mechanics of getting oral discourse translated into marks on the page and, eventually, can learn to produce what is truly written discourse. Once again the adult reads past the handwriting and spelling to guess at what the child wants to say, and children are too busy with the physical acts of calligraphy to worry much about audiences. Anyway, knowledge of audiences in oral situations is largely tacit, and writing invites conscious control. Still, in strange ways the written words are external to the writer, like a person, and thus written language is separate from the children who write. The pleasure of the children in reading last week's writing suggests the degree to which the written experience has grown to be a thing apart, a thing written by someone else despite whatever claims are made for pride of authorship. The older child thus experiences growth and can be analytic about the self that was. Perhaps revision is too much to ask, but Donald Graves is engaged in detailed studies strongly suggesting that revision is an important part of the writing of second graders—providing adults know how to look for it. Even without instruction in revision, the trial-and-error mechanism of successive approximation takes over. The children grow and develop as they discover how to get out of themselves and into language.

Our real concern with literacy, then, is not the sort of competence measured in tests of usage and mechanics, nor even in tests of reading and writing as they are manifested in notes to the repairman or in employment agency forms. We ought to be concerned about literacy in the sense that written language represents our conscious and most refined efforts to say to other people who we are in relation to what we know. Reductionist rationalizations that are preoccupied with the mechanical subskills on the grounds that "you have to start somewhere" or "a journey of a thousand miles has to begin with one step" encourage us to accept our slots in a mechanistic world, to keep our places.

Let me divert your attention for a moment to another use of literacy as it is embedded in the word *literate*. We hear in that second word no subliminal suggestion of *minimum*. Literate people are those who are well-read, cultivated, urbane. These people are probably full of knowledge in general, but even more, they have large views of the world, are able to imagine many kinds of mind, have at hand many plots and elaborations of plots into which they can fit experience. The old image of the education of literate leaders probably included a year of travel on the Continent; I recall Americans in less afflu- ent classes suggesting that a hitch in the military would help young men not merely to shape up but also to dis- cover other kinds of men and thus fit themselves better to be part of the world of affairs. I haven't heard much of that justification in the current political climate. We are retreating into insularity. These days, in my part of rural America, I don't even hear as often that youth should run off to the city in order to grow up. I interpret these prescriptions in whatever form, though, as suggestions that growth requires additional perspectives on one's world, an awareness of what other people are and have been. A text provides information, but information shaped by the purposes of a human will. As we study the mind revealed in the text, we are engaged primarily in discovering the other person in the only way it is accessi- ble to us—in language. Touching is fine, but limited. Even watching does not make sense until the vision is transformed into signs and symbols, systems and catego- ries. The language in its context gives the meaning to touching and seeing just as these in turn give meaning to language. We need the ultimate refinements of literary language to represent most fully the mind in front of us.

In this statement I am not referring merely to poetry or fiction or drama, but to any form of the language in which the full implication of value is emphasized. I suppose I might even stretch so far as to include that "objective" discourse in which the writer makes a great issue of being self-effacing. To declare oneself "transparent" and to deny any evidence of one's own values is a remarkable form of linguistic artistry, and is itself a declaration of value, but it should not be confused with wooden conventionality any more than the bushels of Elizabethan sonnets gathered by Sir Sidney Lee should be confused with those of Shakespeare.

How does one cope with literacy of this kind? I have quite traditional answers. In all discourse, but especially in literary discourse, writers should be simultaneously aware of writing as it represents a content and writing as a thing-in-itself, a system of symbols and signs. A student of writing should always be asked to observe the translucence of the verbal surface, for in that surface is the signal to stand back from the content itself in order to contemplate the situation in which the language exists. Simply, that reminds us to inquire who is sharing language, for what reason. We are made into observers as well as participants. The most obvious examples are in literary language. In the end I suggest that literary language, however conventional or gaudy it may on occasion be, is always antireductive, is always exhibiting human value. For that reason the study of how literary language works is always going to challenge us to deal with the essential competency in language, the one that deals with human relationships.

To be sure, when we meet most of the students in most of our classes we cannot expect literary masterpieces. Our theories of development suggest that if we pose literary problems we will get no more than approximations of literature, but we will engage the student in real choices among the features of language. Still, for most students literary efforts may be overwhelming. Quite likely most of our effort should be spent with writing that defines rather explicitly a scene in which writer and reader act— perhaps quite ordinary transactions of daily existence— for such moments define us all. Even in commonplace activities we shift from direct representations of reality to highly abstract categorizations of reality, and back, and so explore how language defines people.

Now I am back where I began. Until you enter my scene I am undifferentiated as the maker of the world I see. When I oblige myself to talk to you, to imagine who you are and what your world is, then I begin to define myself by finding how we compare and by adjusting to differences. Where are we truly analogues? What is the idea or act that separates us and marks my position as not-yours? The language we share is not quite a common property. Its features are enough alike so that we recognize meaning in them; they are enough different so that each of us must be cautious in interpreting what the other says. I try to guess where our language is not shared and in the process I discover my bias as much as I find yours. And here are the problems of human competency that interest me and, I think, should interest us all. We are not talking about writing as a craft with economic value; we are describing what it means to be human.

I'm not suggesting some standardized test nor even some verbal projective therapy. Rather, I think we should concentrate on devising classroom tasks that really engage a student's commitment to an audience. Who is to care what the student says? Classmates? The teacher as a person of wide experience? The teacher as gradegiver? The teacher as copy editor? Some reasonably well-defined fictional character, such as a customer, a potential employer, a younger sibling, the dean, the sheriff? Just because it is hard sometimes to design a task in which a student may present real knowledge for an appropriate audience does not mean such a question is unimportant. It may mean the proposed task is irrelevant if no one could be expected to care.

When we define the audience, we also define the student. Can some legitimate role in the student's existence be imagined as a proper writer for a given audience? What does it mean to write for the boss? For a dependent? What ethical restraints are imposed? Answering such questions forces self-awareness. The answers may also imply that some subjects are inappropriate because the writer's viewpoint cannot be significant. The purpose of a given communication cannot be realized apart from the general policies of the writer, the stand such a person takes before the work, the conditions of self from which a style emerges. Yet, the policies that define a person's will cannot exist except in relation to specific issues presented to particular people. If the task is constructed without a consideration of such limits, the writing will probably be bad and instruction implied by the task will be false.

Of course, none of these strictures really can be discussed apart from language, so those who allege we ought to be offering vocabulary building, grammar, and copy editing have a chunk of a truth; but in the abstract language is a rarified study. Life exists in the language as it is used, so tests of language apart from uses are sterile, probably misleading. I don't doubt that such tests can discover some competency, but it may be so lifeless as to be useless. The worst part of such tests is that they divert the attention from what we really want to know.

The real problem with our preoccupation with competency expressed in quantitative terms is that the questions we ask establish the limits of useful knowledge. If you ask a foolish question, you get a foolish answer; if you ask a tricky question, you get tricks; if you ask a trivial question, you play trivia. The items are "secure," of course, so no one can really challenge the test, but we quickly learn to define our objectives only in forms which can be tested in standard ways. The theory says we define our objectives before we design the test, but practice is governed by practicability, so we accept the implied limits of the test method. Early in a testing program we may make an issue of what is not reported; we may proclaim that we are only making a predictive correlation with a .4 reliability, but the brief newspaper accounts don't have room to report the qualifications, academic advisers never see the test description, and before long the discussions treat the test domain and scores as the limits of reality. So Lord Kelvin is back. In writing, that means that the relationships and contexts disappear as classroom interests. We no longer ask whether language represents us and our ideas to people we care about. I forget who I am because I deny that I need to know you. That is the tragedy of scoring too many tests.

The University of Iowa

Literacy
part three

Literacy, Culture, and Human Consciousness

A Literal View of Literacy

EDWARD P. J. CORBETT

Edward P. J. Corbett is a professor of English at Ohio State University. His Classical Rhetoric for the Modern Student *(Oxford University Press) was largely responsible for the revival of interest in classical rhetoric among American teachers of composition. Since then he has written or edited more than half a dozen books in which he brings the rhetorical tradition to bear upon modern problems in composition and literature. Corbett was the editor of* College Composition and Communication *from 1974 to 1979 and an associate editor of the* Quarterly Journal of Speech *from 1972 to 1974. Since 1973 he has been a member of the editorial board of* Philosophy and Rhetoric.

In this article Corbett indicates that one of the most basic problems associated with literacy is its definition.

If one wants to get literal about literacy, one has to get back to what is really basic—to the ABC's. As long as a language exists only in the oral medium, people do not need or desire an alphabet. Except for those occasions when we recite the alphabet, we are not conscious of letters when we speak. The alphabet is literally a feature only of the graphic form of the language.

The invention of the alphabet—probably about 1500 B.C.—is commonly spoken of as being the greatest invention of man after the wheel. And indeed it is a monumental invention. But it is conceivable that the alphabet would not have had to be invented. There are languages spoken today that do not have an alphabet or any other system of script. Those languages exist only in the medium of sound. There are some acoustical speech surrogates that do not even rely on verbal sounds in order to communicate. We all respond quite readily to the bells and buzzers of our daily life. Some of us can even make sense out of the dots and dashes of the old-fashioned telegraph key. And Walter Ong has given us a fascinating account of the drum languages of Africa in his *Interfaces of the Word* (Cornell University Press, 1977).

Most of us find it difficult to imagine living in a culture that did not have both a spoken and a written form of the language. But we must remember that inhabitants of this planet lived for hundreds of thousands of years without a written language. And there are still millions of people today for whom the written language virtually does not exist because they do not have access to that form of the language.

Yes, our troubles—or our blessings—all began with the invention of the alphabet. If the written language had remained at the level of the pictograph, we might have blissfully muddled through. Anybody can read pictures. For that reason, an international set of pictorial symbols has been devised for such purposes as warning us not to smoke in a certain area or cautioning us not to enter a one-way street or directing men and women to the right rest rooms. But some busybody had to complicate our lives by devising about two dozen distinguishable squiggles. One can tick off and extol the contributions to civilization that have accrued from this literal invention, but one should not forget that this invention is also one of the reasons why schoolboys and schoolgirls creep unwillingly to school. It is, after all, a taxing effort to run through all the *grammata* from alpha to omega. It is not just language teachers who bug schoolchildren about their ABC's. Parents and employers and editors also nag them about their ABC's and about getting their p's and q's right and about dotting their i's and crossing their t's. There is no relief for the literate from the punctilios of life.

As Marshall McLuhan and Walter Ong have reminded us, we shift dimensions when we shift from the comfortable oral medium to the vexing graphic medium. The spoken language, which appeals to the sense of hearing through the medium of sound, exists in the dimension of time. The written language, which appeals to the sense of sight through the medium of graphemes, exists in the dimension of space. The consequences of that difference in dimensions are enormous. For one thing, sound is evanescent—here today and gone a second after it is uttered. Until the invention of sound-recorders, we had no way of permanently preserving speech. Speech could, of course, be temporarily preserved in someone's memory, but it persisted only as long as that memory could hold it and as long as that human memory continued to exist. It could also be preserved by being translated into written language, if there was a written language to preserve it. But neither the memory nor the script could preserve the sounds that were originally uttered. Thanks to the technology of electronics, we do have a permanent sound recording of the "I Have a Dream" speech that Martin Luther King, Jr., delivered at the Lincoln Memorial in Washington, D.C. Abraham Lincoln's "Gettysburg Address" exists only in printed form.

Existing as it does in the dimension of space, writing, on the other hand, can get a purchase on duration, if not on longevity. Writing is chiseled into stone, etched into the hides of animals, or inked onto paper. Thousands of years later, we still have some of the messages that literate stonemasons chiseled into granite tablets. But the durability of the grapholect (as E. D. Hirsch calls it) has a counterbalancing price. It is more difficult for people to acquire the skills of writing and reading than to acquire the skills of speaking and listening. If we are native speakers of the language, we probably have no memory of the difficulty of learning how to speak our language and how to understand it when we heard others speaking it. We picked up the skills of speaking and listening as part of the normal process of growing up—almost, as it were, by osmosis. "I lisped in numbers, for the numbers came," Alexander Pope once wrote. Unlike Pope, we probably did not naturally start to speak in measured cadences, but we can claim that we began to acquire our oral and aural skills even before we were toilet-trained.

But, oh, the agony of acquiring the other two communication skills, reading and writing. We commonly use the verb *to learn* in referring to our acquisition of speaking and listening: "I learned how to speak and listen." It is equally true that we have to learn how to read and write, but we are accustomed to use the verb *to teach* in connection with those skills: "I was taught how to read and write." Once upon a time, in those primary-school years, there was a teacher—perhaps now forgotten—who taught us how to read, taught us how to decode the black squiggles that were inscribed on the white pages of a book. We did not realize it then, but that teacher, whoever it was, made a greater contribution to our education than any other teacher we ever had afterwards. That teacher gave us an entry into the privileged world of literacy. Millions of people throughout the centuries since the invention of the alphabet have lacked that enabling teacher, and as a consequence, the world of script and print was forever closed to them. Even more millions of people have never learned, were never taught, how to write.

The point of all of this is that the skills of reading and writing do not come to us naturally. We have to make a conscious and strenuous effort to acquire them. And thereby hangs a tale. A huge network of schools has had to be established, and legions of teachers have had to be trained and enfranchised, to assist young people in the acquisition of skills that do not come to them as part of the natural process of growing up.

How vital are the skills of reading and writing in our society? Are they indispensable or just important? Are they a necessity or a luxury? Any group of people seriously concerned about the problem of literacy in our society has to seek some kind of answer to questions like those. Since the teaching of reading and writing entails an enormous expenditure of effort on the part of many people, we had better determine, at least to our own satisfaction, that the benefits are worth the costs.

Before we seek for answers to those questions, however, we should determine what we mean by the term *literacy* or the privative term *illiteracy*. Most people understand *literacy* to refer to the ability to read and write. *Illiteracy*, by corollary, signifies the inability of someone to exercise one or both of those skills. But those definitions do not reveal the degrees of literacy or illiteracy that exist. The extreme illiterate is the person who cannot read or write anything in his or her native language. Such a person cannot even read a street sign or endorse a check. For such a person, reading and writing are totally inaccessible channels of information or expression.

Those are the people who are commonly referred to as being "functionally illiterate." But that term is also sometimes applied to people who can read but cannot write or vice versa. And the term is even applied to people who can read and write but not well. That latter group too embraces a wide spectrum of competencies. At one end of the spectrum are those who can discriminate street signs and can write their own names on an application form but cannot make much sense out of the instructions written on a can of insect repellent or cannot pen an intelligible note. At the other end of that spectrum are students—college freshmen, for instance—who their teachers claim cannot comprehend most of the expository essays in their anthologies of readings or cannot consistently write in complete sentences.

If we are at least aware that different people have different notions of what constitutes illiteracy, we can demand or supply a stipulative definition of the term whenever we are engaged in discussions of the subject. Before we could answer the question, How necessary is literacy for survival in our society? we would have to establish a stipulative definition of *literacy* and maybe also of *survival*.

What if we are speaking about that group of people who cannot read or write anything? Can they survive in an urban environment in the twentieth or twenty-first century? If we mean by *survive* "continue to live or exist," we have to answer, "Of course they can." Thousands of illiterates of that sort live to a ripe old age even now. Millions of such illiterates in previous centuries survived in teeming cities, at least until malnutrition, disease, or back-breaking work did them in. But what if we mean something less extreme when we use the verb *survive*? What if we mean something like "prosper" or "flourish" or even "do well"? Now we are getting down to the core of the matter. We are getting close to the line that English teachers have always preached when they were trying to induce their students to work hard at their reading and writing.

Even if we have not observed firsthand the lives of those who cannot read or write anything, it does not take much of a stretch of imagination for us to conclude that such people do not do very well in our society. Yes, we could all tell our own tales about businessmen or entrepreneurs, past or present, who could not write their own names but who directed with marvelous efficiency the fortunes of their multimillion-dollar corporations. But such prospering illiterates are rare in a modern industrial society and are rapidly becoming rarer. The more usual fate of those who cannot read or write is deep-pit poverty and gnawing shame. Even now, some 41 million American adults earn less than $5,000 a year, and most of those are people with little schooling and even less proficiency in reading and writing (*New York Times*, Sept. 9, 1979, pp. 1, 37).

Accurate figures about the number of illiterates in a nation or even in a single large state or city are hard to come by, but those estimates that are based on some kind of survey, such as a census, are at least reliable. The estimate one most often sees for the United States is that one out of every five adult Americans—about 23 million people—can be classified as functionally illiterate. Those figures include those who cannot read or write anything, as well as those who have minimal skills in reading and writing but cannot apply those skills to everyday tasks. Even so, it is staggering to learn that in a country that has had universal education for most of the twentieth century, millions of citizens cannot handle reading and writing well enough for those skills to be of help to them in performing some of the tasks of day-to-day living.

The statistics about the state of illiteracy in the world are even more staggering. In 1977 UNESCO published its report on the extent of illiteracy in 179 countries and territories for the thirty-year period from 1945 to 1974

(*New York Times*, April 30, 1978, p. 23). According to the UNESCO report, the world illiteracy rate dropped from 44.3 percent to 34.2 percent between 1950 and 1970. But owing to the population explosion in the world during the same period, the absolute number of illiterates rose from 700 million in 1950 to an estimated 800 million today. Because in most countries women have less access to schooling than men do, women today account for 60 percent of the world's illiterates.

Figures like these boggle the minds of those of us who have been literate for as long as we can remember. We find it hard to imagine what it must be like not to be able to read or write. But we can learn to empathize with illiterates for their disability by recollecting our experiences with the foreign languages we may have studied in school. If we took any foreign languages in school, we may still have a fairly serviceable reading knowledge of those languages, but we probably share in the usual dismal record of Americans in writing, speaking, and comprehending those languages. If we have been tourists in Europe, we know firsthand how frustrating and humiliating it is not to have even an elementary proficiency in the language of the host country. If we have had that experience, we have a sense of what it is like to be functionally illiterate in one's native language. If we have visited a country whose written language does not even use the Roman alphabet that we are accustomed to—for instance, an Arabic script—we have some sense of what it is like not to be able to read or write *anything* in a language.

Literate people need comparative experiences like these to be able to realize what a handicap it is to be deficient in reading or writing a language and to realize what a tremendous gift it was to have been given the opportunity to acquire those valuable skills. Comparative experiences like these are also salutary because they make us realize that people who do not have a functional proficiency in the reading, writing, speaking, and listening skills of a language are not necessarily stupid. They may just be victims of deprived circumstances.

While it is well for us to be aware of the crippling nature of functional illiteracy and of the staggering number of illiterates in the world and in our own nation, the truth of the matter is that those of us who teach on at least the secondary or college level seldom if ever encounter students with such severe deficiencies. People who cannot read or write seldom get as far as the high schools, and they never go on to college. Mina Shaughnessy once told me that even after the CUNY system opened its doors to all graduates of New York City high schools, she never had to cope with a total illiterate in any of her classes. What she had to deal with, and what all of us who teach on at least the high school and college level have to deal with, are students who for one reason or another have not attained a sufficient level of proficiency in reading or writing to ensure that they can handle their academic work well enough to qualify for graduation. These students are indeed disadvantaged, but they are remediable. The remedy, the repair, the removal of their linguistic deficiencies, is the challenge that faces us as teachers.

How many of our students today fall into the remedial or remediable category? Has the number of them been increasing in recent years? The mass media would have us believe that the number of verbally deficient students has grown alarmingly in the last ten years or so. Reports of scores on national tests seemed to corroborate the claims about the decline in verbal proficiency. The most dramatic and most widely publicized of these reports was the College Board's announcement of a forty-nine-point drop in the average verbal score on the Scholastic Aptitude Test, from 478 in 1963 to 429 in 1977. A recent news story in the *New York Times* (September 9, 1979, p. 1) reported that in 1979 the average SAT verbal score again dropped two points, to 427.

So serious did the College Board regard this decline that it appointed a twenty-one-member advisory panel, chaired by Willard Wirtz, former Secretary of Labor, to study the data in order to interpret it and perhaps discover the reasons or the causes for the decline. The advisory panel published its report in September of 1977 under the title *On Further Examination*. The panel concluded that the decline was unmistakable and serious, and had to be attributed to a complex of causes, not to any single cause. It declared that about half of the decline, at least up to 1970, could be attributed to the changing composition of the college-bound population. Not only did an increasing number of students go on to college during the period under study, but a larger percentage of students with low high-school averages were going on to college. The advisory panel identified six other developments that contributed, in various degrees, to the decline in verbal scores: (1) the proliferation of elective courses during those years; (2) a diminishing seriousness about the learning process, as reflected in excessive absenteeism, grade inflation, and adulteration in the reading level of textbooks; (3) the increase in the number of hours that young people devoted to watching television; (4) the changing structure of the American family; (5) the social and political disturbances of the late sixties and early seventies; (6) a marked decline in the motivation to learn.

Many of the findings of the blue-ribbon advisory panel may strike us as being commonplace and predictable, but for the most part, the conclusions and interpretations of the panel were restrained and sensible. At every point, the panel took great pains to hedge their generalizations with carefully thought-out qualifications, and in the conclusion of the report, the panel urged that "a broader look be taken at the whole picture—including whether we are testing in the best possible way whatever ought to be tested."

What a number of professional organizations, including the National Council of Teachers of English, objected to publicly was the implication that the incontestable evidence of a decline in verbal scores on objective tests was also an indication of a decline in students' writing ability. While conceding that there could be some correlation between verbal aptitude and the ability to compose a piece of connected discourse, the professional organizations kept insisting that the most reliable way to test writing ability was to elicit a piece of writing from the students during the testing period. (It is noteworthy that the College Board and some of the other national testing agencies have restored the writing sample to their testing procedure.)

One of the liveliest controversies sprang up over the question of whether there was a demonstrable decline in the composition skills of students. Even English teachers differed in their assessment of this situation. Many English teachers proclaimed vociferously that the writing skills of their students had gone to hell in a basket—and they maintained that they had files of student themes to substantiate their claims. Richard Ohmann, on the other hand, former editor of *College English*, said in an article in the *Chronicle of Higher Education* that he thought all the hullabaloo about the state of student writing had been created largely by the mass media. I myself publicly maintained that I did not find student writing to be noticeably worse than it was five years ago, ten years ago,

fifteen years ago. I claimed to have found the same pro-
portions of excellent writers, average writers, and poor
writers as I had ever found. But without substantiating
evidence, my opinion about the situation does not de-
serve any more respect than the opinion of any other
veteran teacher of writing.

In response to the oft-repeated complaint that "Johnny
can't write" (an echo of *Newsweek's* often cited cover story
of December 8, 1975), Richard Lloyd-Jones wrote an article entitled "Is Writing Worse Nowadays?" for the April
1976 issue of the *Spectator,* an alumni magazine of the
University of Iowa. In this article, Professor Lloyd-Jones
asks three questions about the complaint, questions
which on the surface seem to be simple-minded but which
really get at the heart of the matter: "First, who is Johnny?" In other words, what particular segment of the
student population are you talking about when you say
that Johnny can't write? "Second, what is writing?" Are
you talking about the physical act of making marks on a
piece of paper or about spelling and punctuation or about
the ability to reason and to develop ideas cogently and
coherently? "Third, what does *can't* mean?" Are you talking about Johnny's ignorance of the subject-matter being
written about or about Johnny's lack of skill in articulat-
ing his thought? These probing questions really disclose
how complex rather than simple, how vague rather than
clear-cut, is the charge that students can't write any-
more. As Lloyd-Jones says, "We just don't know much
about writing in bulk lots."

One agency that made an attempt to do an inductive
study of student writing in bulk lots was the National
Assessment of Educational Progress (NAEP). This agency did a comparative study of the writing produced by
nine-year-olds, thirteen-year-olds, and seventeen-year-
olds in 1969 and again in 1974. What the comparative

study revealed was that the 1974 students were no better or worse than the 1969 students when it came to the mechanics of writing—spelling, punctuation, grammar, and usage. The 1974 students were noticeably inferior to the 1969 students, however, when it came to the organization, the coherence, and the adequate development of their ideas. A number of surveys circulated recently among the faculties of various departments in the schools seem to confirm these findings: it is the cognitive skills associated with the writing process that have noticeably declined, not the editing skills.

Whether students today are less adept at writing than students of a decade ago may still be a moot question, but one beneficent effect of all the clamor about the state of student writing is that the composition class has been granted an upgraded status in the curriculum. At a time when enrollments in literature courses are declining precipitously, students are flocking to writing courses—frequently on their own initiative. And teachers of writing are now getting some of the attention and rewards that they have always deserved but did not always get.

If there is indeed a solid, rather than just a fashionable, renascence of interest in rhetoric and composition, maybe we can do something to improve the writing skills of *all* students. I say "maybe" because there are those who claim that the art of writing cannot be taught—at least, cannot be taught under the circumstances in which it has been traditionally taught in our schools. But despite the perennial skepticism about the effectiveness of the writing course, the course has maintained a prominent position in most curricula and, as I have said, seems now to be strengthening that position. The skepticism about the effectiveness of writing courses will persist in spite of the growing enrollments, but perhaps we can find reason to be optimistic in the fact that English teachers are now a great deal more sophisticated about the teaching of composition than they were ten or fifteen years ago.

A number of developments in recent years have contributed to the growing sophistication of teachers of writing. For one thing, many English departments are now offering formal courses in rhetoric and the teaching of composition for prospective teachers. Formerly, they entrusted that training to the colleges of education or set up rather haphazard weekly practicums for their own beginning teachers of composition. As a result of these newly instituted graduate courses in rhetoric and composition, there is a growing sense of professionalism among teachers of writing and less need for teachers of writing to learn by trial and error.

Another healthy development is that English teachers have overcome their reluctance to turn for help to other disciplines, like psychology, psycholinguistics, anthropology, communications theory. In the last five years the professional literature about the teaching of writing has been filled with the names of internationally known scholars in physics, psychotherapy, cognitive psychology, and cultural anthropology—names like Thomas Kuhn, Carl Rogers, Lev Vygotsky, Michael Polyani, Jerome Bruner, Jean Piaget. Exposing themselves to the insights from these other disciplines has also helped English teachers to overcome their suspicion of the scientists' ways of conducting empirical research and testing hypotheses. One of the journals now published by the National Council of Teachers of English is called *Research in the Teaching of English.* In articles that appear in that journal, English teachers do not just *assert* that some new method of teaching composition has dramatically improved student writing; they now present quantitative and qualitative evidence to corroborate their claims.

Teachers of composition have also profited from the use of the system of error-analysis that was largely developed by teachers of English as a second language. ESL teachers are interested not so much in the specific errors that foreign students make in speaking and writing English as in the *reasons* for the errors. This system does for the teaching of writing what miscue analysis does for the teaching of reading. The rationale is that if teachers can discover the reasons for the errors, they can provide the specific kind of instruction and exercise that will help students overcome or avoid their difficulties with the new language. The most brilliant presentation of this system for English teachers was Mina Shaughnessy's *Errors and Expectations: A Guide for the Teacher of Basic Writing* (Oxford University Press, 1977). In this book, Professor Shaughnessy reported on the study that she and her colleagues did of the writing of the thousands of disadvantaged students who descended on the various branches of the City University of New York in 1970, when that system adopted a policy of open admissions. This book is generally so well known now among teachers of writing that it does not need any extensive review from me. I have said publicly before, and I will say again, that this is the best book on the teaching of writing to be published in this century—maybe the best book ever published on the teaching of writing. Anyone who reads this book and absorbs the insights and recommendations that it offers will grow a whole cubit in stature as a teacher of writing.

One further development seems likely to enhance our effectiveness as teachers of writing. I refer to the attempts at a number of schools in the last two to three years to involve the faculty of all departments in the teaching of writing. Some of these attempts to enlist the whole faculty in the teaching of writing have been generously funded by grants from the federal government or from private foundations. Four of the most publicized of these programs are the ones at Beaver College and West Chester State College in Pennsylvania and at Michigan Technological University and the University of Michigan. These and other programs are exploring ways to induce all teachers to require some writing from their students and to train busy subject-matter teachers in how to evaluate student writing quickly and reliably. For years, English teachers have complained that they cannot persuade students to take writing seriously if other teachers do not require writing and do not base at least part of the students' grade in the course on the quality of the writing displayed in examinations and course papers. If some of the approaches and techniques developed in these funded programs prove to be readily exportable to other schools, we may be able to enlist the cooperation of our colleagues and to convince students that competency in writing pays dividends in settings other than just the English classroom.

My title promised a literal view of literacy. I have been literal, and I have also been pedestrian and unoriginal. What I have presented is a tissue of what has oft been thought and said on the subject of literacy. I have cultivated the obvious and reaped the commonplace. I have not offered any solutions to the monumental problem of literacy in the world or even in our schools, but I have suggested that we may be more effective in the future in combating at least the remediable kind of deficiency in writing.

I am somewhat ashamed that I have not had anything useful or optimistic to say about the much more serious kind of illiteracy, the deficiency in reading. I find the state of reading among our young people to be much more alarming than the state of writing. And of course if the reading does not improve, it is not likely that the writing will improve. The times do not seem propitious for a wholesale improvement in reading skills. Television and other audio-visual media seem likely to preempt more rather than less of the time of our young people. The decline of attention among young people, the increasing absenteeism in the schools, the atmosphere of violence that prevails in some of our urban schools are signs of the time that do not give promise that our young people will expend the effort needed to develop their skill in reading. I am profoundly sad about the prospects. Just on the score of the pleasure that I have derived from reading, I feel sorry for what our young people will miss out on if they abandon books. But maybe they will find nirvana in other pursuits. If they do, they will have to experience that nirvana firsthand, rather than vicariously, through reading. I wonder if they will ever stand "silent upon a peak in Darien," as I have many times done while reading a book. 'Tis a pity. But we always think that people are to be pitied if they do not have what we have had. Maybe we can staunch our bleeding hearts by recalling that paradoxical maxim that we literate people have often read in print: "Ignorance is bliss." Wouldn't it be ironical if we were to discover that literacy, after all, is the source of all our woes?

The Ohio State University

Luria on Literacy: The Cognitive Consequences of Reading and Writing

FRANK J. D'ANGELO

Frank D'Angelo is a professor of English at Arizona State University. He is widely respected for his numerous theoretical articles about composition and rhetoric, and particularly for his books A Conceptual Theory of Rhetoric *and* Process and Thought in Composition, *both published by Little, Brown.*

In this article D'Angelo reviews the work of a number of psychologists, with particular emphasis on A. R. Luria, whose field work was conducted in 1931 and 1932 but not available in English until 1976. Luria's work would seem to indicate that the acquisition of literacy radically alters perception and cognition, with important consequences not only for individuals but also for entire political and social structures.

It is often claimed that in an electronic age literacy is only marginally important, and therefore educators ought to be more concerned with media literacy than with reading and writing. Those who hold this point of view argue that young people spend more time with television and other nonprint media than they do with written forms of expression. They assert that many people leaving school today will seldom need to read or write except in the simplest forms that will enable them to cope with everyday tasks. Most of their communicating will be done by word of mouth. Even if these contentions were true, I would argue that literacy would still be important, for literacy makes possible modes of thinking that cannot be acquired in any other way.

In contrast to the kinds of abstract, conceptual thinking found in literate people, the kinds of thinking associated with nonliterate people is concrete and specific, embedded in a particular situation. Such thinking tends more toward the sensorimotor and perceptual than toward the conceptual. Once, however, literacy is acquired, the way the individual perceives reality undergoes radical restructuring. Perception goes beyond immediate sensory experience as direct impressions are put into a system of abstract linguistic categories. Thinking on the basis of classes, similarities, and cause-and-effect relationships becomes more abstract and theoretical. There is a dramatic transition from sensorimotor and perceptual thinking to propositional thinking. The thinking of nonliterate people, however, evidently does not advance beyond the level of what Piaget calls the stage of concrete operations.

Literacy enables individuals to conceptualize, to generalize, to draw inferences, and to work out logical relationships among ideas in ways that would otherwise be impossible. The most important forms of cognitive activity, such as perception, classification, comparison, cause and effect, and deduction, change noticeably as a result of literacy, and it is with these modes of thinking that I will be primarily concerned in the remainder of this paper.

One of the most basic processes of cognitive activity is perceptual thinking. Literate people tend to perceive different kinds of mental events as discrete. Among literate people, perceptual experience is differentiated. The mental life of nonliterate people, however, is not highly differentiated. Things do not stand out as discrete and fixed as they do in the thinking of literate people. For example, on the sensory level, seeing, hearing, feeling, tasting, and smelling are closely related so that a specific stimulus will not only arouse a corresponding sense, but may also arouse related senses.[1]

Another basic process of cognitive thinking is classification. Literate people classify objects and events according to some abstract logical or linguistic principle. They base their classifications on qualities or attributes that can be mentally detached from their objects. Nonliterate people base their classifications on the perceptual configuration of objects that appear together in a realistic situation. The Bakairi Indians of Brazil, for example, use the same class-word for emerald green, ultramarine, and cinnabar red. It should be apparent that the grouping of these colors could not be based on an actual similarity. Instead, the grouping of these colors is naturalistic. The word used to designate these colors has been taken from the name of a parrot that bears them all. Australian aborigines use the same word for thirst and water. Their word for wood and their word for fire is likewise the same.[2] These examples illustrate the extent to which the classifications of nonliterate people are embedded in the concrete activities of daily life.

Perhaps the richest source of contrasts between literate and nonliterate cognition is the study conducted by the Russian psychologist A. R. Luria in 1931 and 1932, but not available in English until 1976. Luria and his assistants went to remote parts of the Soviet Union to test nonliterate people in various cognitive tasks, including the grouping of similar objects. These people were peasants whose ancestors had been virtually nonliterate for centuries. Because they lived in an area with a backward economy, an extensive network of schools was opened up for them, and literacy programs were set up to familiarize them with modern technology.

When given the task of grouping similar objects, Luria's subjects invariably arranged them according to some functional activity, a grouping that literate people might describe as idiosyncratic. These peasants saw no need to use abstract or linguistic categories. Instead, they grouped objects according to the roles they might play in the daily work experience.

For instance, one peasant was shown a picture in which there were three wheels and a pair of pliers. When he was asked if these objects were alike in any way, he responded: "No, they all fit together. I know the pliers don't look like the wheels, but you'll need them if you have to tighten something in the wheels." The subject was then shown a drawing in which there was a glass, a saucepan, a pair of spectacles, and some bottles, and asked which ones should be grouped together. He replied: "These three go together, but why you've put the spectacles here, I don't know. Then again, they also fit in. If a person doesn't see too good, he has to put them on to eat dinner." In both instances, the objects were grouped together on the basis of their functions in a practical situation. Luria is quick to point out that this kind of concrete thinking is not to be considered inferior, nor is it genetically determined. Most of the peasants involved in this experiment, after a brief training in literacy, could easily shift from situational thinking to abstract thinking, the kind of thinking apparently best suited to a technological culture.[3]

In tests designed to get these same nonliterate subjects to detect similarities, tests clearly related to the process of classifying objects, Luria's subjects seemed unable to detect resemblances between the simplest of objects.

Luria explains why this might be so. In addition to the ability to discern similarities, the process of comparison presupposes the ability to analyze, that is, to isolate and abstract features of the objects to be compared. Citing the classical studies of Binet and other psychologists as evidence, Luria comments that individuals can pick out differences in objects long before they are able to detect similarities. For in order to determine how two objects differ, all one needs to do is to describe the physical attributes of each object. Because the finding of differences depends more on immediate perception and visual memory than it does on linguistic ability or abstract logic, it is easier to differentiate than to mark similarities.

In this experiment, Luria was primarily interested in trying to determine whether a nonliterate person's approach to comparison involved logical or linguistic abilities. Therefore, this test involved two groups of subjects: one literate and the other nonliterate. Each group was asked to compare objects that were clearly dissimilar or objects that might be difficult to incorporate in a practical scheme. As might be expected, the literate subjects assigned objects to a general category. The nonliterate subjects, however, described each object, giving a detailed account of its function, all the while insisting that they had nothing in common.

One of Luria's subjects in the test to detect similarities was a thirty-eight-year-old illiterate peasant, who was asked: "What do a fish and a crow have in common?" He replied: "A fish—it lives in the water. A crow flies. If the fish just lays [*sic*] on top of the water, the crow could peck at it. A crow can eat a fish but a fish can't eat a crow." He was then asked, "Could you use one word for them both?" His reply was, "If you call them animals, that wouldn't be right. A fish isn't an animal and a crow isn't either. A crow can eat a fish but a fish can't eat a bird. . . . A person can eat a fish but not a crow." The subject, unable to find a common term to describe the crow and the fish, reverts to a description of differences.[4]

The process of defining a concept is an operation that is clearly logical and linguistic. It is one of the most basic processes of cognitive thinking. In this test of mental abilities, Luria's subjects were asked to give names for commonly used objects as well as for more abstract concepts. When confronted with these tasks, they either refused to define a concept, saying that it was silly to define things whose meaning was perfectly obvious, or they defined it by using tautologies (e.g., a tree is a tree). Another method they used to define was to tell how something operated. A final method was to describe the object's physical appearance. It never seemed to occur to Luria's subject that they could clarify an idea by defining it.

In this test, one of Luria's subjects was a twenty-two-year-old peasant. When he was asked to explain what a tree was, he rejected the need for explanation and answered: "Why should I? Everyone knows what a tree is, they don't need me telling them." When pressed further to try to explain the concept, he retorted: "There are trees here everywhere; you won't find a place that doesn't have trees, so what's the point of my explaining?" In reply, he was told: "But some people have never seen trees, so you might have to explain." Apparently exasperated, he tries to explain by pointing out features. "Okay. You say there are no trees where these people come from. So I'll tell them how we plant beetroots by using seeds, how the root goes into the earth and the leaves come out on top. That's the way we plant a tree, the roots go down." Finally, when asked how he would a define a tree in two words, his response was to enumerate specific kinds of trees rather than to define: "In two words? Apple tree, elm, poplar."[5]

Another basic process of cognitive thinking is perceiving cause-and-effect relationships. Literate people tend to divide phenomena into causes and their effects. Nonliterate people tend to think of causes and effects as parts of a continuum. Literate people are more interested in why something comes into existence than how it comes into existence. Nonliterate people are more interested in how.[6]

The cause-and-effect explanations of literate people tend to be scientific, that is, they are hypothetical, abstract, and objective. The cause-and-effect explanations of nonliterate people tend to be descriptive and narrative. If asked, for example, to explain a very simple phenomenon, such as why the turtle has a flat shell, nonliterate people will tell a story—an etiological tale of origins or a myth. The logical relationship of cause and effect is implicit in the imaginative story, but it is not differentiated. The nonliterate person does not abstract these relationships in a specific, logical form. If asked to explain the phenomena involved in a sunset or sunrise, the literate person will give a scientific explanation. The nonliterate person, however, will tell a story, personifying the sun as a being who leaves his cave in the morning and returns there at night.[7]

One of the most important processes of cognitive thinking is making inferences and drawing conclusions based on schemes of logical thinking as represented by the syllogism. The use of the syllogism represents an advanced state in the development of cognitive acitivity. In a less advanced state of cognitive development, direct impressions play a more important part than the use of abstract schemas. The abstractness of the syllogism does

not correspond closely with immediate experience. Yet
there is a distinct advantage in using this abstract mode
of reasoning. The syllogism permits the individual to
draw conclusions from given premises without having to
draw upon immediate, concrete experience.[8]

As he did in his experiments to try to determine what
principles nonliterate people would apply in classifying,
detecting similarities, and defining, Luria devised experiments to determine how the parts of a syllogism
would function in the thinking of nonliterate peasants,
what kinds of inferences and conclusions they would
draw, and how these inferences and conclusions would
interact with their practical experience. The subjects
were given a syllogism and asked to repeat it in order to
determine if they perceived the individual propositions
as parts of a whole or as individual judgments. Then they
were asked to make the appropriate deductions. The
content of some of the syllogisms was taken from the
peasants' practical experiences. The content of others
was deliberately separated from practical experience so
that they would be forced to make inferences by logical
deduction alone.

Twenty people took part in the experiment. Fifteen
were nonliterate. Five, who had received a short-term
education, were chosen for comparison. Those subjects
who had some training in literacy could grasp the overall
structure of the syllogism. They could also see the logical
relationship between the major and the minor premise.
The nonliterate subjects, however, could not perceive the
logical relation of the parts of the syllogism. They tended
to see each proposition as an isolated judgment. They
repeated each proposition as if each were a separate sentence, completely unrelated to the others. They dis-
trusted premises not based on personal experiences, and
they refused to use these premises for subsequent reason-

ing. Or they ignored the premises altogether and attempted to reason from immediate experience.

In one experiment, Luria's subjects were given the following syllogism: "Precious metals do not rust. Gold is a precious metal. Does it rust or not?" The first subject tested, an illiterate peasant who was eighteen years old, responded by repeating parts of the syllogism: "Do precious metals rust or not? Does gold rust or not?" A second subject, this one barely literate, also repeated parts of the syllogism: "Precious metals rust. Do precious metals rust or not?" A third subject not only repeated parts of the syllogism, but he also added words that were not part of the original: "Precious money rusts . . . there was something else, I forget. Do precious metals rust or not?" Luria's conclusion is that these subjects did not perceive syllogisms as logical systems. Instead, they repeated parts of the syllogism as if they were unrelated. When they did repeat the premises, they rephrased them, making them specific rather than universal. As a consequence, they were unable to use the premises to draw the necessary conclusions.[9]

As part of this experiment, a thirty-seven-year-old peasant from a remote Kashgar village was given this syllogism: "In the Far North, where there is snow, all bears are white. Novaya Zemlya is in the Far North and there is always snow there. What color are the bears there?" Failing to make inferences from the syllogism, the subject replied: "There are different sorts of bears." The syllogism is then repeated and a different response is elicited: "I don't know; I've seen a black bear, I've never seen any others. . . . Each locality has its own animals; if it's white, they will be white; if it's yellow, they will be yellow." With this response, the subject appeals to personal, visual experience. He was then asked: "But what kind of bears are there in Novaya Zemlya?" He respond-

ed: "We don't talk about what we haven't seen." The
syllogism is repeated again, and he is asked: "But what
do my words imply?" He responded: "Well, it's like this:
our tsar isn't like yours and yours isn't like ours. Your
words can be answered only by someone who was there,
and if a person wasn't there, he can't say anything on the
basis of your words." The questioning then goes on at
some length with the same results.[10]

On the basis of this experiment, Luria concludes that
nonliterate subjects can make valid judgments about
things that concern them directly. But when they are
asked to turn to a system of theoretical thinking that is
divorced from a practical situation and that depends on
linguistic, logical thinking, they fail to make the necessary inferences.

In general, Luria concludes that cognitive processes
change qualitatively, as a result of literacy, and in changing they radically alter our perceptions of reality. As
Luria puts it:

> The generalized way in which reality is reflected . . . undergoes
> radical restructuring. The isolation of the essential features of
> objects and the assignment of objects to a general category of
> objects with the same features ceases to be regarded as some-
> thing minor and insignificant. New, theoretical thought opera-
> tions arise—analogies of the properties of things, assignment of
> them to abstract categories, and so forth. Thinking processes
> begin to involve more and more abstraction and generalization.
> Theoretical "categorical" thought begins to function in addition
> to operations of practical "situational" thinking and occupies a
> more prominent place, sometimes beginning to dominate
> human cognitive activity. Gradually we see the "transition from
> the sensory to the rational". . . one of the most important as-
> pects of the development of consciousness.[11]

Luria's research is, of course, almost fifty years old,
and it was conducted, as he admits, without the advan-

tage of more recent refinements in cultural psychology. But his conclusions are reinforced by views expressed more recently by other psychologists. Jerome S. Bruner, for example, claims that literacy fosters in the individual something he calls "analytic competence," by which he means an ability to apply complex problem-solving strategies and thought patterns to "linguistic representations," "propositional structures," and "ensembles of propositions" that are quite different from the objects and events of direct experience. This ability, Bruner tells us, is metalinguistic in that it usually requires and invents "new notational systems like mathematics, or more powerfully elaborated forms of the natural language like poetry."[12]

Even those who might accept Luria's findings, however, may not be entirely sympathetic with his inferences and assumptions. One scholar with serious reservations about what he calls "the literate bias of schooling" is the psychologist David Olson. Olson argues that it is simply not true that all knowledge can be translated into words. Nevertheless, he contends, schools operate on that premise, and as a result, the primary aim of schooling is to make people literate. Olson comments that there are two kinds of knowledge: common-sense knowledge and scientific knowledge. Common-sense knowledge is "coded for action." It emphasizes the particular and the concrete. Its most important tools are illustration and example, rather than classification, deduction, and inference. Common-sense knowledge is laden with values. It is more concerned with the social context than with the context-free elaboration of ideas. Scientific knowledge is better suited for reflection than for action. It emphasizes universal laws, and its most important tools are explanation and prediction. Scientific knowledge is relatively value-free, being more concerned with ideas than with social values.[13]

Olson goes on to say that schools emphasize scientific knowledge at the expense of common-sense knowledge. But, he contends, if all knowledge cannot be translated into words, then literacy is simply a means to a specific kind of knowledge that has its own biases, not knowledge in general, not universal knowledge. Olson concludes that there are some kinds of practical activity that can be taught informally. Literacy may be a means to achieve some goals, but it may be an inappropriate means for practical actions that are embedded in immediate contexts and it may not be the best medium for exploring novel ideas or personal feelings.[14]

Not all scholars agree with Olson that an excessive reliance on the written word has a constricting and distorting effect. They point out that language has functions other than those used to convey common-sense knowledge and scientific knowledge. Such a view of literacy, they claim, leaves the place of literature and those humanities that rely on the written word unsettled. Rather than being constricting, the humanities liberate the imagination and allow literate persons a glimpse into the human condition. As to the charge that literacy may not be the best medium for exploring novel ideas or personal feelings, one critic argues that, in fact, quite the reverse is true:

> The expressive possibilities offered by being able to write thoughts down after mature consideration would seem, on first principles at least, to be a friendly condition for linguistic innovation. In fact the advent of literacy, far from extinguishing the imagination, has vastly increased the number of its expressive options. Indeed, it is hard to overestimate the subtle reflexive effects of literacy upon the creative imagination, providing as it

does a cumulative deposit of ideas, images, and idioms upon whose rich and appreciating funds every artist enjoys unlimited right of withdrawal.[15]

Another perspective on the relationship between language and cognition is provided by sociolinguists like William Labov, who questions the value that some scholars have ascribed to abstract, theoretical modes of thinking and to middle-class verbal habits. He does admit that illiterate people ought to attain minimal linguistic skills, but he wonders how much ability in handling abstractions is really necessary for individuals in some cultural groups, and he suggests that some kinds of verbal behavior may even be dysfunctional. He contends that many middle-class speakers and writers unnecessarily complicate their syntax, and qualify and temporize to such an extent that they lose their audiences in a maze of detail. He denies that highly complex thought is as flexible and subtle as some psychologists say it is. In many ways, he contends, working-class speakers are more effective speakers and reasoners than middle-class speakers. Labov also argues that nonstandard dialects, which depend more on oral modes of thinking than on literacy, contain logical, syntactical, and semantic distinctions that are perfectly adequate for the needs of their speakers.[16]

But, as Bruner argues, it is not the possession of logical, syntactical, or semantic distinctions in language that matters, but rather *the elaboration of their use.* "Given the concrete, intuitive use of language, limited to matters of fact, one seems . . . to go no further than Piaget's concrete operational phase in which one deals in concrete events in a logic that is *ad hoc,* local rather than universal, probabilistic, and not based on propositions related to each other by a principle of logical necessity."[17]

Bruner goes on to declare that it is only when "one uses language beyond this 'minimum' level that it alters or, indeed, transforms the nature of the thought processes in a special way. The most general specification of such language use is its *movement toward context-free elaboration*."[18]

Perhaps the most disturbing questions about the relationship between literacy and cognitive development have been asked recently by Sylvia Scribner and Michael Cole.[19] Based on their studies of the Vai society of Liberia, Scribner and Cole have raised serious doubts about the generalizations made by those developmental psychologists who believe that literacy leads inevitably to dramatic changes in cognitive abilities.

The Vai are a West African people who invented a syllabic writing system about 150 years ago. With this system they write letters and keep records. A few of the Vai keep diaries and record clan histories and tales. For the most part, however, reading and writing are not a prominent part of their activities. Because this writing system is not learned in school as part of formal education, Scribner and Cole had a unique opportunity to study the effects of literacy on cognitive development separately from the effects that formal education might have on intellectual development.

Their research left them with two different conclusions. On the one hand, it demonstrated "that skills involved in literacy behaviors are indeed transferable to behaviors unrelated to literacy . . . that what an individual does with text, or with pencil and paper, can promote specific skills that are available to support other behaviors." On the other hand, they did not find "that literacy in the Vai script was associated in any way with generalized competencies such as abstraction, verbal reasoning, or metalinguistic skills." Scribner and Cole

conclude "that the effects of literacy, and perhaps schooling as well, are restricted—perhaps to the practice actually engaged in or generalized only to closely related
practices."[20] But they caution their readers that they are
generalizing on the basis of very skimpy data and that
they are a long way from resolving the two conflicting
viewpoints, the one contending that education is specific
in its effects and the other maintaining that it develops
general abilities.

It would be narrow-minded indeed not to agree in part
with the criticisms of Labov, Olson, Scribner, and Cole.
Nonliterate and illiterate people have considerable intelligence, and many can outperform their literate counter-
parts in a variety of practical and cognitive tasks. If
many of us were placed in a different environment among
nonliterate or illiterate people, our behavior would probably be considered unintelligent. Cognitive differences
are almost certainly a result of different environments
and educational opportunities. Yet the ability to conceptualize and to handle abstract symbols is absolutely necessary in a technological society. A lack of these skills
may be enough to consign many citizens in American
society to lives of hopeless deprivation.

Arizona State University

Notes

1. Heinz Werner, *Comparative Psychology of Mental Development*,
rev. ed. (Chicago: Follett Publishing Co., 1948), pp. 87–88.

2. Ibid., pp. 225–26.

3. A. R. Luria, *Cognitive Development: Its Cultural and Social
Foundations*, trans. Martin Lopez-Morillas and Lynn Solotaroff, ed.
Michael Cole (Cambridge: Harvard University Press, 1976), pp.
53–56.

4. Luria, *Cognitive Development*, pp. 81–82.

5. Ibid., pp. 86–87.

6. Werner, *Comparative Psychology*, p. 307.

7. Ibid., pp. 304–7.

8. Michael Cole et al., *The Cultural Context of Learning and Thinking* (New York: Basic Books, Inc., 1971), p. 231.

9. Luria, *Cognitive Development*, pp. 102–6.

10. Ibid., pp. 107–9.

11. Ibid., pp. 162–63.

12. Jerome S. Bruner, "Language as an Instrument of Thought," in *Problems in Language and Learning* (London: Heinmann, 1975), p. 70.

13. David R. Olson, "The Language of Instruction: The Literate Bias of Schooling," in *Schooling and the Acquisition of Knowledge*, ed. Richard C. Anderson et al. (Hillsdale, N.J.: Lawrence Erlbaum Associates, 1977), pp. 71–72.

14. Ibid., pp. 86–87.

15. Jonathan Miller, *Marshall McLuhan* (New York: The Viking Press, 1971), p. 104.

16. William Labov, "The Logic of Nonstandard English," in *Language and Social Control*, ed. Pier Paolo Giglioli (Harmondsworth: Penguin Books, 1963), pp. 92–93.

17. Bruner, "Language as an Instrument of Thought," p. 70.

18. Ibid., pp. 70–71.

19. Sylvia Scribner and Michael Cole, "Literacy without Schooling: Testing for Intellectual Effects," *Harvard Educational Review* 48 (November 1978): 448–61.

20. Ibid., pp. 456–57.

Reading, Technology, and Human Consciousness

WALTER J. ONG, S.J.

*Walter Ong, S.J., is the William E. Haren Professor of
English and Professor of Humanities in Psychiatry at
St. Louis University. He is also a past president of the
Modern Language Association.* One of the recurrent
themes of his work is the way in which various media—
whether oral poetry, writing, print, African drum
languages, or television—alter the noetic habits (that is,
the perceptual and cognitive styles) of the people who
use them. He has often focused on the differences
between the noetics of cultivated oral societies, such as
the Greece of Homer, and highly literate societies, such
as the Greece of Aristotle; his work has encouraged
contemporary writing teachers to view their beginning
students as nonliterate rather than illiterate, and to
understand the cultural and psychological chasm they
must cross if they are to participate in the consciousness of literate communities.

*In this essay, Ong combines his interest in these
noetic differences with his awareness of recent trends
in literary criticism on both sides of the Atlantic, in
which common-sense assumptions about how the
written word makes meaning—or rather, how readers
make sense of the written word—are being challenged.
Part of this paper was delivered as the opening address
for the Ferguson Seminar on Publishing at the College
of William and Mary, November 17–18, 1977. The full*

text was published in England in The Yearbook of
English Studies *10 (1980): 132–49, and is reprinted
here with permission of the* Yearbook *editors and the
author.*

I

In the United States and Western Europe the past decade
has seen an unprecedented development of a highly intel-
lectualized interest in reading and readers. This interest
has thus far been relatively elitist, quite distinct from the
concurrent distress over practical reading skills and
more unprecedented than this distress, for, as historians
of education well know, dismay over lack of reading skills
and other language skills has been a normal and even
fashionable mood in academia over the centuries. The
newer interest in reading and readers springs from theoretical rather than practical concerns, although its implications for practical pedagogy can be, or can become,
quite real.

An indication of the present state of affairs could be
seen at the December 1976 convention of the Modern
Language Association of America in New York City,
when the Forum on the Reader of Literature attracted an
audience of around 1000 to 1200 persons (transients
make exact figures impossible). Hundreds of these pur-
sued the reader question still further in one or more of
the six satellite workshops that continued discussion of
the subject through the rest of the three-day convention.
The forum itself was billed as providing "A New Perspective in Criticism and Teaching" and proposed as its focal
topic, "Do Readers Make Meaning?" Strategic wording,
raising teachers' hopes and flattering readers, a self-

consciously depressed majority, as well as titillating dabblers in subjectivism.

Most persons at the forum, however, were there not for wish-fulfillment but for more informed and sophisticated reasons. Collectively, they had been reading or hearing of works published in the past decade or so by members of the *Tel quel* circle in France such as Roland Barthes, Philippe Sollers, Tzvetan Todorov, and Jacques Derrida. They knew something of the Heideggerian and Husserlian thought that lay back of these works, something of the related phenomenology of discourse developed by Paul Ricoeur and by the late Maurice Merleau-Ponty, probably less about the earlier phenomenologist Louis Lavelle and the much earlier and precocious Maine de Biran, a great deal about Ferdinand de Saussure's linguistics and Claude Lévi-Strauss's linguistic and anthropological structuralism, as well as about the Russian and Prague formalism decanted and matured in the work of Roman Jakobson, and something about the French psychoanalytic cultural critics Michel Foucault and Jacques Lacan. The forum attendants were also often deeply into Henry James's and E. M. Forster's reflections of fiction writing and into the work of American critics and literacy theorists emerging from or diverging from the old New Criticism, such as Wayne Booth, Robert Scholes, and Robert Kellogg, who discuss the nature of narrative as such—what can be done to develop a story line out of the welter of lived existence—and they had become acquainted with the views of cisatlantic critics in dialogue with the French such as Harold Bloom, Geoffrey Hartman, Paul de Man, J. Hillis Miller, and E. D. Hirsch, Jr., and with some of the work of hermeneuticists and theorists from the German milieu, such as the Polish-born Roman Ingarden or Hans-Georg Gadamer, Erich Kahler, and Wolfgang Iser. Most of the audience had read

work by members of the forum panel themselves: David
Bleich, Stanley Fish, Norman Holland, Walter Ong, and
Michael Riffaterre. (Besides these panelists, some of the
other persons just mentioned here were also present at
the forum as members of the audience, and entered into
the discussion.)

All this is quite a mix of persons and of public and
private epiphanies, even without the many more names
that could be added to those above, but nothing less could
give an adequate idea of the complex intellectual milieu
out of which the present interest in reading and readers
has emerged. The discussion of readers and reading often
runs deep, intellectually and psychologically. I present
here some suggestions on the discussion and some hypotheses as to why at the present moment of history
questions about the reader and reading so fascinate literary critics, philosophers, linguistic analysts, psychologists, and others.

II

Some of the basic considerations that in this milieu
mark discussion regarding reading and readers can be
stated as follows. The wording here is my own.

1. Reading is a special kind of activity and cannot be
understood as simply an activity parallel to listening.
(Like many other observations entering into the discussion, this observation has been confirmed by the clinical
and experimental work of psychologists, whose ranks
could furnish other names assimilable to those just mentioned.)

2. Writing and reading establish a special situation
marked by absences, gaps, silences, and opacity. Faced
with a text, readers find that both the author and original

context are absent. Readers themselves have to produce the equivalent of both—the equivalent, for they can produce neither author nor context in total actuality. The context is no more, and the author, often enough, is dead.

3. "The writer's audience is always a fiction." This, a chapter title in my recent book, *Interfaces of the Word*, is my own way of focusing some of the issues involved in reading and writing, including some of those noted here below. As contrasted with a speaker, a writer normally addresses persons who are not present and who indeed must be absent. I am writing a book that, I hope, is going to have a hundred thousand readers, so please, everyone get out of the room. I want to be alone. I must imagine my readers, most of whom I shall never know, must imagine and set up a certain mood for them, imagine the literary traditions they are used to so that they can introduce what I am writing into their own imaginative world— and my readers must be able to match themselves to what I have imagined for them, or my writing will not work. This fictionalizing of readers is not entirely arbitrary on the part of the writer. He or she must provide readers with models that real readers are used to or can adjust to readily.

4. Reading, one might say, is always a preterite activity. It deals with something that is over with. Texts come out of past time. They are things, not events. Conversation is never a preterite activity. It is an event, not a thing.

5. Texts all have to be "naturalized" or related to a present known form of communication, related to what people talk about now or can talk about. There are synchronic problems of naturalization: a novel by John O'Hara is more readily naturalized by most present readers of novels in the West than one by Robbe-Grillet. And there are diachronic problems: because of differences in

time and culture, it is not easy for present-day readers to naturalize *Piers Plowman,* even in a modern English version, unless the readers are specially trained. Otherwise they have trouble deciding what is going on.

Another way to say this is to say that texts must be interpreted. Interpreting a text means inserting it somehow into the ongoing conversations you live with. No matter how difficult of access the meaning or meanings in a text from an unfamiliar milieu may be, no matter how bizarre, the text has to be related in some way to what the reader knows of actuality, if only by contrast, or it cannot be understood at all. The Latin-derived *interpretation* (etymologically, trafficking, negotiation) is the equivalent of the Greek-derived *hermeneutic* or *hermeneutics* (which has, however, a divergent etymology). Hermeneutics is fashionable today, as it never has been since Aristotle got together—or somebody got together— his *Peri hermeneias (On Interpretation).*

6. Interpretation, which all texts require because they are things coming out of a past, actualizes potential meanings (implicit, unconscious, etc.) submerged in the text, making the text more fecund than oral utterance can normally be (unless the oral utterance is recorded, which is to say, made into a text). For all utterance has submerged meanings, unconscious as well as conscious elements. Total explicitness is impossible. Meanings submerged in an oral utterance can be surfaced by questions put on the spot to the speaker—that is, the speaker can be forced to interpret his own remark just made. But, unlike oral utterance, which is present to one audience at a given time in a given place, a text is present potentially to a limitless number of audiences, that is, to a limitless number of readers, to any individual who undertakes to engage the text at any time and in any place after the text is inscribed. Thus the written or printed text demands

interpretation on a scale of an entirely different order than most oral utterance ever does.

7. Texts exist in relation to other texts much more than in relation to spoken language. This relationship is often labeled *intertextuality,* a term which is obviously related to the intersubjectivity dear to phenomenologists and which thereby reveals some of the phenomenological sources and alliances of textualist study. Another way to think of this situation is in terms of literary tradition or even literary history. However, present discussion of intertextuality has advanced far beyond earlier, and necessarily vaguer, understandings of tradition and history. Those who studied literary history and tradition in the past, when discussion had not progressed so far as it now has, were unable to articulate its psychological or metaphysical or phenomenological underpinnings so precisely as can present-day thinkers. Literary scholars even as recent as Hippolyte Taine or George Lyman Kittredge, not to mention earlier writers, really could not explain so well as we can today the basis of their passion for comparing works of literature with each other. They tended to halt at simply noting likenesses and differences, not always knowing entirely what to make of either.

8. A text has to create its own world in the consciousness of the reader. This is particularly true of what we style "literature" in the narrow sense of this term, creatively imaginative writing, but it is true of all texts— even, to take an extreme example, of a bank draft, which normally, in the United States, sets up in the consciousness of readers a world where (with some assistance now from computers) the text or draft is propelled relentlessly into a federal reserve bank and thence to the bank on which it is drawn, with certain consequences for two or more parties. Even so laconic a text as "No left turn" on a

traffic sign belongs to a special world, rather different from that of the bank draft, as both are different from the normal world of informal conversation. An itinerant from Mars would soon learn that "No left turn" is part of a world of police, courts, fines, and jails, while "Keep off the grass" belongs normally to another world, whatever the size of the lettering.

Literature, in the narrow but common sense of imaginative, creative writing, sets up the most complex and various worlds of all (which may very well include in their manifold the specialized worlds of bank drafts and traffic signs together with that of informal conversation). The novel and its derivatives can set up probably the most complex of these literary worlds, such as the world of Dickens's *Pickwick Papers,* or that of Proust's *A la Recherche du temps perdu,* or that of Virginia Woolf's *To the Lighthouse,* or of Joyce's *Finnegans Wake.* Because its world can be so exquisitely massive and dense, the novel can in certain ways stand as a paradigm of all writing and as the roomiest drawing board on which problems regarding readers' attitudes are displayed. Many of the scholars named above focus their discussion and theories on novels.

9. Language is among other things structure, and literary form is structure, and readers as well as hearers are engaged in interpreting structure. Nevertheless, no utterance is ever totally structured in fact, even unconsciously, however much structure, conscious or unconscious, may be found in it or imputed to it.

The spirit or ghost of structuralism moves through much of the discussion I have been referring to. This structuralism derives ultimately in great part from the linguistic work of Ferdinand de Saussure (1857–1913) and the related linguistic and anthropological work of Claude Lévi-Strauss. Structuralism itself is a polyvalent phenomenon, analyzing language, myths, kinship systems, and human behavior, in patterns often reducible to diagrams that seem to enter simultaneously into a vast diversity of fields from grammar to psychoanalysis and thus to unite these fields. Despite its complexities as a vaguely but effectively unitary phenomenon, structuralism is clearly a particular manifestation of a major development in consciousness today that is represented also in systems analysis and the development of the computer. Like the computer, structuralism works basically with binary oppositions, and, also like the computer, it can generate almost without limit details that can be variously illuminating, stimulating, dazzling, dizzying, or dull—sometimes all these at once.

Elsewhere I have undertaken to point out that concern with the concept of system as such is a typical product of noetic structures, encouraged by print, that tend to apotheosize closed systems—in Cartesian philosophy, for example, and Newtonian physics, as well as, most spectacularly of all, in Sir Isaac Newton's remarkably labored and stillborn theology, recently studied by Frank E. Manuel. Present-day systems analysis, however, is intimately aware of the impossibility of totally closed systems, most acutely in the life sciences and social sciences. As is advertised in the title of Anthony Wilden's book *System and Structure: Essays in Communication and Exchange,* this awareness modulates systems analysis from concern with closure into a study of communication; that is to say, a study of the interactions between systems (or, in the case of human persons, between quasi-systems), all of which are in one way closed and in another way open.

Literary structuralism and anthropological structuralism, although related to systems analysis, are often less reflective about the limitations of the models they use than is straight systems analysis. However, the limitations of all structuralism are real and permanent. For, while it is helpful and at times virtually indispensable for the kinds of understanding of man needed today, structuralism often suffers from the same problem that many structures in the physical world themselves suffer from: it often exists in a chronic state of imminent collapse. Linguistic structuralism is on mostly solid ground, but critics such as Alan Dundes are fond of pointing out that both literary and anthropological structuralism rely on a somewhat arbitrary selection of certain elements and a neglect of others in literary works and in myths in order to discern the structural patterns they find so exciting. Moreover, as Jonathan Culler notes, "Structuralism cannot escape from ideology and provide its own foundations" (p. 253), and in this way is thus no better off than competing modes of analysis, whatever its distinctive and invaluable contribution to understanding may be.

III

Much more could be said about current discussion of reading and readers. But enough has been said, I hope, to indicate the range and intensity and relative novelty of current fascination with the subject. How is this widespread phenomenon to be accounted for?

In many ways, of course. But basically, I believe, our fascination with the psychodynamics of reading can be understood as a stage in the evolution of human consciousness, that is, in the evolution of mankind's way of relating the human interior to the exterior world and to itself. Man is an interiorized being from his beginning: a being who can say "I" is inextricably involved with his or her own interior, exquisitely aware of the interior that he or she is and that no one else can directly enter or savor. No other human being knows or can know what it feels like to be me. This interior self-knowledge, self-savoring, marks man off from other living animals. But the human interior, the "I," is also keenly aware of the exterior world and involved in it: without this involvement, interior consciousness cannot become aware even of itself.

Evolution of consciousness takes place as negotiations proceed between interior and exterior and, via the exterior, between the human interior and itself. Evolution of consciousness is characterized at root by the growth of consciousness out of the unconscious, by raising into the world of conscious awareness more and more of what had been earlier related to only unconsciously. Consciousness grows phylogenetically: the longer mankind lives on earth, the more of the earth and of mankind's own life comes under conscious understanding and planning. Growth in consciousness in one age is normally handed on to the next. Consciousness grows ontogenetically: adults act more out of reflective, conscious awareness than children do. In the course of growing up, each human being learns to establish awarenesses and to form concepts to which the particular circumambient culture and language give access, and in doing so appropriates into himself or herself the past of the species lodged in the concepts, culture, and language. Thus, in the evolution of consciousness, ontogeny and phylogeny are intimately related—even more intimately, it would seem, than in biological evolution, for consciousness is not only formed out of the past but can reflect on itself and its own ontogenetic and phylogenetic past, and grow further in consciousness out of such reflection.

In its overall pattern, the evolution of consciousness is marked by an increasing articulateness not only about the external world but particularly about consciousness itself. The New Testament writers were more articulate about the human interior than were the compilers of Genesis. The later Greek plays of Euripides are more articulate about interior problems of conscience than were earlier Greek plays. The faculty psychology running from ancient Greece through the Renaissance, with its intellect and will and memory and various sense faculties and virtues and vices, was more articulate about man's interior than the mythology that had gone before, but nowhere so articulate as the depth psychology that has succeeded faculty psychology.

In *The Inward Turn of Narrative* Erich Kahler has shown in detail how, at least in the West, as consciousness evolves over the centuries, narrative is concerned less and less with the outside world as such and more and more with interior consciousness. Eventually, interiorization in narrative reaches a kind of absolute. Narrative works that are most representative of today's advanced states of consciousness, such as for example *Finnegans Wake,* can often be read as stories not only about interior consciousness but also about interior consciousness dealing with itself in the totally interiorized act of composition in writing—which, although it aims ultimately at exteriorization, is of itself one of the most self-consciously secret, if not absolutely the most self-consciously secret, of all secret human actions. Present-day concern with writing, and complementarily with reading and readers, reflects the present deep interiorization of consciousness.

Writing and reading are not only deeply involved in this always intensifying interiorization process that marks the evolution of consciousness but are also in fact a part of the process. Without writing and print the interiorization of consciousness that marks modern man could not have taken place. In his classic *Preface to Plato* Eric Havelock has shown how an oral culture tends to identify the knower with the exterior known object in a kind of participatory noetic, and how writing, a solitary activity, as reading paradigmatically also is, sets off the observer from the observed and throws consciousness back on itself.

It is no accident that the discussion of reading and the reader has grown out of or alongside phenomenology and psychoanalysis which have developed conceptual apparatuses for delving into consciousness and its substructures, the subconscious and the unconscious, and into human interiority generally, with an articulate directness impossible in earlier ages. French structuralists such as Lacan or Barthes or Derrida have made the connections between interest in psychoanalysis and interest in writing and readers—the focus of Derrida's *grammatologie*—utterly explicit.

Concern with reading and the reader has grown also with and out of today's concern with communication, a concern all but obsessive not only in highly technologized countries but also in most if not all the technologically developing countries around the world—as I myself can attest from personal experience in lecturing in Arab countries, in subsaharan Africa, and in Latin America, as well as at international conferences elsewhere attended by persons from technologically developing countries around the world.

All human communication is an interiorizing operation, though much of it may be less interiorizing than might be desired. In its fullest sense communication is more than the mere movement of information, imagined as a commodity shuttled through a medium from one point to another in a field. Human communication proceeds from the interior consciousness of one human being to the interior consciousness of other human beings. To utter means to "outer," to externalize what has come into being within. And we utter something, "outer" it, only so that someone else can interiorize it again, take it into his or her own interior consciousness, know it, appropriate it, bring it into the inner realm of awareness where each of us is alone, where each says "I," where each knows that he or she is and knows. Mechanical models for communication processes such as are used in information theory are helpful, but are all grossly deficient and of themselves misleading because they have no way of representing the interiority essential to all human communication—the individual, personal consciousness itself, utterly different in each one of us. Human beings are open closed-systems, externalizing interiors, retaining their interiority inviolably in the act of externalizing, of uttering. They are irreducible to models because they are simpler than anything we can devise to represent them. No matter how much I explain everything I know, including myself, you still cannot discover what it feels like to be me. I am simpler and clearer to myself than any explanation. Explanation only muddies the waters

The current interest in communication—which is not without antecedents, notably the pervasive interest in rhetoric from antiquity to the Romantic Age—is itself evidence of growth in interiorization. Of all forms of verbal communication, chirographic and typographic communication—the use of writing and print—is in many ways the most deeply interiorizing. Both writer and reader, as has already been noted, work typically in isolation. Production of a printed text of course calls for cooperation of groups of persons, but print isolates writer and reader from one another even more than writing does, putting each on his or her own. Professional writers work in solitude, where they address absent persons virtually all of whom are and always will be totally unknown to them, and readers have to create all alone in their own minds the utterances of authors whom they will never know and, indeed, who in many cases have long been dead. The press is commonly taken to be one of the mass media, along with radio and television, as of course it is, but it differs from these in its enforcement of loneliness. Thirty persons simultaneously reading copies of the same book side by side in a library do not constitute a group of the sort formed by thirty persons listening to the same direct, live, oral presentation or even to the same taped oral presentation on radio or on television. Sound forms community as reading alone cannot.

Analysis requires disengagement, distance—both real and psychological. Reading distances. By distancing the reader strategically both from his material and from those who are speaking to him about it, reading fosters analytic management of knowledge, "objectivity," as oral communication alone cannot. The psychological consequences of the reader's situation are enormous. A study by George Gerbner and Larry Gross of the Annenberg School of Communication at the University of Pennsylvania has shown that most heavy television viewers (65 percent) are prone to believe the society they live in to be far more violent than it in fact is, but if TV viewers are also regular newspaper readers, their estimates of violence in real life today are far lower and more in accord with actuality—and this despite the fact that newspaper readers are fed with their own quotient of zealously collected and professionally highlighted violence. Even under unfavorable conditions, reading encourages, or at the very least is congenial to, disengagement, analytic objectivity.

IV

Much more could be said about the interiorization enforced by reading, and about the cultural gains and losses that the practice of reading entails. For cultural gains all involve losses. This is the story of human existence and of maturity. We must die to one stage of existence if we are to move on to the next. Writing entailed both the death of the old orality and the realization of previously hidden potentials of the word. There can be no doubt that for the advance of human consciousness, for its greater actualization, writing and reading, with the interiorization they implement and enforce, have been indispensable, absolutely required. For the fuller meaning and the fuller implications of this statement, I can only refer to works of my own and of others on this subject. But one special connection between writing and consciousness I should like to attend to here, namely, the technological connection.

Our growing understanding of the psychodynamics of writing and reading reveals the depth of mankind's involvement with technology as nothing else can. Technology has affected the externals of man's lifeworld immeasurably, from the realm of mechanical gadgetry to the realm of living organisms. But with the development of writing and its sequels, that is, print and electronic management of knowledge, technology has fused with human consciousness itself.

It is not difficult to be aware that printing presses, like computers, are technological devices, although it may be surprising and remains somewhat mysterious that the first assembly line in human history, the first mechanical arrangement to produce complex products made up of replaceable parts, each single product and part exactly like every other, was the printing press. One might suppose that the first assembly line would have been set up to manufacture objects satisfying physical needs, perhaps peaceful, perhaps polemic—set up to manufacture ploughshares or swords—rather than to deal directly with the needs of the mind. But that is not the way it was. Mass-production technology comes into being by producing the printed book.

It is a little more difficult to become aware that writing itself, which preceded printing from movable alphabetic type by about five thousand years, is also a technology or at least demands a technology. Although an unworked pebble or stick and an unprepared surface can be used for the most primitive production of minor bits of script, as soon as writing becomes more than occasional boondoggling, it requires specially prepared surfaces (clay tablets, wax tablets, skins, paper) and specially prepared instruments (styli, brushes, pens, paints, inks). With such external, technological equipment, the mind can undertake kinds of activity impossible for it previously. The analytically organized treatise, such as Aristotle's *Rhetoric* or *Physics,* can come into existence. There is no way for an oral culture to go through the kind of elaborately analytic thinking processes that constitute such works. The only way for someone in an oral culture to produce a lengthy treatise on physics would be simply to recite it extempore. This has never been remotely possible. Oral cultures produce lengthy and magnificent verbal and intellectual performances, but these are "stitched" together, "rhapsodized" (*rhaptein,* to sew; *oidē,* song) formulaically and thematically, not analytically. With writing one can put something down, move on, return to what is written, rearrange, and ultimately develop an elaborately logical, causal, analytically sequential explanation. This constitutes a new kind of noetic structure, not realizable until the mind had interiorized writing, made writing part of the support and fabric of its own intellectual procedures.

As writing reorganizes noetic structures, so does print. Through the development of the index and other means of rapid visual retrieval, print detaches knowledge from utterance as such far more decisively than writing and makes knowledge into something like a commodity. Early preprint encyclopedias such as the *Etymologies* of Isidore of Seville or the *Speculum* of Vincent of Beauvais are perceived largely as collections of sayings: knowledge is essentially associated with something that someone has said, with utterances. An *Encyclopaedia Britannica* article today, produced for and by print, does not typically strike the reader as a series of utterances, although this in fact is what it really is, but rather as a block of knowledge, a commodity, which can be located by tracing through a series of places—an alphabetized entry in a directory to locate a library, card catalog in the library to locate the encyclopedia, alphabetized entries in the encyclopedia to locate the particular article by volume and page. The ultimate in this reduction of knowledge to place is of course the computer, with its infinitely complex but more purely mechanical retrieval, which works by sorting out localized bits of information.

Technologies dealing with the word all lend themselves to deep interiorization, including computer technologies. We appropriate them into ourselves. It is virtually impossible for thoroughly literate persons to imagine a word as pure sound totally divorced from its mechanical representation in letters. The technology of writing has been irretrievably incorporated into consciousness. Writing and print have been so deeply interiorized that we normally are unaware how much our ordinary noetic processes depend on them. Knowledge processed in oral fashion strikes technologized man as unusual, perhaps strangely charming: Khalil Gibran's utterances, commonplaces in an oral culture, seem exotically beautiful to those whose thought processes are shaped not in this oral fashion but by writing and print. The computer is rapidly becoming comparably interiorized. Many persons today habitually set up problems and find answers in computerized form with no sense of doing anything that is not completely natural, not a part of ordinary thought processes. And we have similarly interiorized, assimilated, the other auditory electronic media that have introduced us to the new age of secondary orality—that of radio and television, both dependent on writing and print for their existence and use. These media also have restructured our noetic processes and our sense of presence to ourselves and to the universe in ways that are new but already so much a part of us that they are as transparent as words themselves.

The presence of the new technologies within human consciousness, from writing to electronics, is complicated or enriched by their interaction with one another. For a new medium does not destroy earlier media at all, but reinforces them and at the same time utterly transforms them. The use of writing does not suppress talking, but encourages more of it, if only because there is more to talk about. But writing changes the way people talk. Once the mind has become familiar with extensive analytic thinking through the use of writing, it becomes possible to proceed orally to some degree in analytic fashion. And indeed it becomes on occasion obligatory to do so. Now, talk must echo written performance to some extent: one must not only write but also speak in a literate—that is, lettered—mode.

Similarly, print reinforces the use of speech and of writing but transforms them. James Joyce wrote *Finnegans Wake,* but he wrote it to be a printed work. Its style is that not of a writing culture but of a print culture. Joyce's carefully elaborated idiosyncrasies of spelling and word formation, which are integral to his style, would be unenforceable and in effect unthinkable before print, for a manuscript culture could not effectively reproduce such idiosyncrasies in thousands of copies. Joyce's originally written verbalization for his readers is dependent upon a sense of a text that is fixed in a way which only typography makes possible. That is to say, as he composes, Joyce feels himself forming typographically fixed text. His writing is typographic writing. It is exquisitely oral, too: it invites being read aloud, and is most poignant when so read. But in it the persistent orality of the Irish heritage has interacted with print and is utterly transformed by print at the same time that it is being intensified. No tales about Cuchulain ever sounded quite like *Finnegans Wake*. They were not constructed, not thought out, that way.

In similar ways, electronic verbalization, particularly through radio and even more through television, is affecting our present speaking and writing and printing styles, and thus our modes of thought, without at all doing away with talk or writing or print. Thus, for reasons still somewhat mysterious, television favors thought and expression that is, or is presented as, impromptu and informal. Typographic cultures find this fitting, for, despite its name, television is quite insistently oral—some of its most typical shows are simply "talk shows"—and typographic cultures inevitably come to associate orality with informality. Primary oral cultures, on the contrary, typically associate oral performance not with informality but with formalism. The taste for impromptu informality encouraged by television feeds back into the other media: our writing and printed publications today commonly affect informality to a degree unknown in earlier ages, and not merely in fiction but also in other texts. Today even official documents seldom achieve the suffocating ceremonial decorum common to documents in the past, when the ceremonial formality fostered in oral cultures was taken over by scribes and other writers and made even more heavily ceremonial (again, a new medium always reinforces the older, though it eventually transforms it). Washingtonese may be stiff, but its formality is relaxed compared to the curial style of the Vatican, a relict of the more oral distant past.

But even the curial style is changing. Today's psychological structures and thought processes favor writing and print that are more "natural," which means impromptu and informal, as we, paradoxically and inaccurately, imagine oral performance normally to be. The bewildering feedbacks here show how complexly reinforcements and transformations are effected when new and old media interact.

V

When we treat of the interiorization of the technologies of writing, print, and electronics, we should remind ourselves that the appropriation of technology by consciousness, like everything else in human development, has its own special dangers. The principle danger is that instead of appropriating technology to consciousness we may appropriate consciousness to technology. Deep familiarity with complex technologies encourages taking machines as models for everything; ultimately it encourages thinking of consciousness itself as simply a technology and even of the human being as a kind of machine. It is distressing to see otherwise sophisticated persons fall into this simplistic trap, blindly and with a kind of joy.

To make machines even moderately convincing as models of consciousness, you have to leave out a lot, most notably the center of consciousness itself, the sense of "I" earlier mentioned here, which each human consciousness has in its unique way—the source and boundary of all in me that counts most, that reduces to no model, to nothing else at all, but is simply itself, inaccessible except from within. Yet the effort to conceive of man, including human consciousness, in terms of a machine model to the exclusion of this "I" is made over and over again in the biological sciences or in psychology or sociology or information theory, despite the patient and convincing demonstration of the futility of all such efforts on the part of specialists such as the biologist Paul A. Weiss or the neurophysiologist Sir John Eccles, or the neuropsychologist Karl Pribram, and others.

Man and machines are more intimately related than most persons think, but in no simple way. In the perspectives being developed here, we must keep in mind that when technology is interiorized through writing and print and electronics, man does not by that simple fact become mechanized. Rather, when technology is interiorized, machines are humanized. Technology not only transforms consciousness and noetic processes but is itself transformed by consciousness. When we speak of technology as operating within the mind, we are speaking of something that is no longer purely a machine, but of something living, generative, producing results—including, at times, new technologies—which technology outside the mind is totally incapable of generating. Life envelops and enlivens the unliving.

VI

Infinitely more could be said about the interactions of technologies with and within consciousness, but I have perhaps said enough to suggest some of the ways in which noetic processes and psychic life generally are complicated by the technological transformation of the word that we know as writing, print, and electronics. The point here is of course that the complications have taken place within the psyche rather than in the outside world. All technologies—the processing of wood and metal, textile work, bridge building, automobile manufacture, chemical industries, and so on—affect man's interior sense of his lifeworld, his sense of himself in relation to the universe, and thus enter into human consciousness to change its structure. But nowhere does technology enter into the structures of consciousness in man's interior life so intimately as when it is used to transform the word itself by means of writing, print, and electronics. For the word comes from the interior: to touch it is to touch consciousness directly.

Present-day attention to the reader and reading, or complementarily, to the writer and writing, is attention to the interior world of consciousness as transformed by writing and print. When Jacques Derrida calls for a science of grammatology, he is insisting quite rightly that to study human thought processes of the sort he attends to, we have to study the nature of writing. And in doing so he is focusing attention on a stage in the gradual interiorization of the human psyche, and the interiorization of the external world within the human psyche that marks human history—which ultimately is not the story simply of wars and conquests and empires or even of economic and social developments, but rather the history of human consciousness itself, no less.

However, for all its excellences and the wide perspectives it opens, Derrida's account, like almost all phenomenological or structuralist or psychoanalytic-structuralist accounts of reading and writing, fails to take into consideration in historical or psychological depth where writing came from. The tradition that Derrida represents derives much of its theory from Husserlian and Heideggerian sources, which have little if any contact with work in diachronic noetics and which consequently lack certain historical and psychological dimensions. It works from analysis of literary texts, mostly recent, post-Gutenberg: Jean-Jacques Rousseau is a favorite. That is to say, the tradition does not attend in depth to the thought processes of primary oral cultures, out of which writing finally emerged, and consequently suffers from an unconscious chirographic and typographic bias. Most theorists in this tradition show minimal knowledge, if any at all, of the psychodynamics of oral thought processes and of primary oral societies and institutions. These have been worked out at great depth and in meticulous and exciting detail by American scholars, notably the late Milman Parry, Albert B. Lord, and Eric A. Havelock, as well as the many younger scholars associated with them and their work. The psychodynamics of primary oral thought processes form the historical and phenomenological base of all subsequent developments, including writing and print, because they lie at the root of thinking itself, even now.

The relationship between primary orality and writing is paradoxical, for primary orality has been discovered and described by literates, and had to be. Any kind of scientific or scholarly study of anything necessarily involves writing: it produces and advances through texts and the kind of thought processes impossible without texts. The result of this situation is that it is easy for linguistic study to be chirographically biased. For the literate, literature (writing, texts) is the verbalization most accessible to study. It is natural for scientists and scholars to fixate on written language as the paradigm of all language, or at least as the most basic or interesting or powerful form of language. We did not have to wait for grammatology to set up this chirographic focus. Grammar had a similar bias. It had originated as the science not of language as such but specifically of writing, of texts: *techné grammatiké* in ancient Greek meant the "art of letters" (*grammata*, "letters of the alphabet")— the etymology of the term shows the initial focus of the art. And in fact the textual use of language remained the focal concern of grammar until modern linguistics began deliberately to attend to language in a fuller sense, that is, to the spoken as well as the written word. Grammatology is more vocal about texts as texts, but its concerns are in this sense simply those of traditional grammar itself, writ large. (From antiquity in the West oral performance had been studied, too, in the art of oratory or rhetoric— *techné rhetoriké*, "the art of public speaking"--but rhetoric had been concerned with ways of convincing an audience, not with linguistic structure, as grammar had. Until modern linguistics, there was no art that scientifically addressed itself to the structures in ordinary, oral, demotic talk.)

Although the initial focus of language study, the focus on texts rather than on oral performance, reveals a chirographic bias, this bias itself has a certain justification: writing confers on speech vast powers inaccessible to orality, including, as we have seen, the power to reflect scientifically on speech itself and to achieve detailed understanding otherwise unrealizable. Orality can give no explanatory account of itself. Only through the succeeding and secondary phenomenon, writing, can full reflective access be had to the antecedent phenomenon, oral speech. Writing, moreover, can give reflective, scientific access not only to orality but to itself as well. If reflectivity, self-consciousness, and the peculiarly intense interiority that self-consciousness entails are distinctively human, and they are, then writing is in some ways more human than the spoken word.

But this is not to say that the succeeding phenomenon, the more evolved phenomenon, is either more fundamental than the antecedent phenomenon or independent of it. Writing is primary for the kinds of thought that are possible only through writing. But it is secondary in that it depends, ontogenetically as well as phylogenetically, on antecedent orality. This fact is spectacularly and persistently and ubiquitously assertive, diachronically and synchronically: all physiologically and psychologically normal human beings learn to speak in the process of moving out of infancy toward maturity (*infans* actually means "non-speaker," from the Latin *in-*, "*not*," and *fari*, "to speak"). Oral speech wells up out of the unconscious. Most normal children in the past, and millions still, have never learned to write at all: writing did not come into being as oral speech did. Rules for transcribing words into writing have to be consciously devised. They lie at the surface. The rules for the use of language, on the other hand, for grammar in the enlarged sense that encompasses oral as well as written speech, lie so deep that the combined energies of structural and transformational and all other sorts of linguists in the world have never been able to surface them all even for one language, and presumably never will be able to. (Rules for *composing in* writing, as against rules for transcribing speech into writing, of course also lie deep, as suggested in Section II above.)

A major problem for linguistics today is the problem of probing the unconscious. The difficulty in responding to the problem in the way the Husserlian and Heideggerian tradition has thus far responded to it is that this tradition has restricted itself to plumbing the unconscious of literates. Astonishing archeological discoveries have been made. But how about the unconscious of the oral psyche, on which the literate is founded—and founded much more complexly in our day than in the past? For children and even infants of today are subject to massive unconscious influences from the literate world that they have not yet consciously entered. Excavations into the oral psyche are even more astonishing than those into the literate psyche. And the digs have been opened by the psychohistorical sort of work already mentioned, done by Parry, Lord, Havelock, and others who have paralleled or followed them. Phenomenology of language that does not take into account the depth structures of oral noetics is no longer adequate, historically or otherwise, diachronically or synchronically.

Failure to take into account these same depth structures of oral noetics and the subsequent technological transformations of the word by writing, print, and electronics can result in blind spots also in the most sophisticated literary criticism today. Few critics today even advert to certain facts that are salient. The development of the tight, linear, standard plot is the product of writing; before writing, the episodic plot is the universal rule for lengthy narrative. The Greek drama and the kind of plot and characterization it features are the result of writing: the Greek drama and subsequent drama in the same tradition depend on memorization of a text, a composition in writing, which is specially devised to allow for reconversion into oral utterance that is seemingly more or less spontaneous. Tight linear or standard plot does not develop in lengthy prose narrative anywhere in the world, so far as I know, until print has been interiorized in the psyche—some three centuries after its invention.

The fully "round" character of the sort E. M. Forster discusses develops only in a print economy. The noetic processes encouraged by the Romantic Movement of the late eighteenth century and later depend on print. And so on.

But we have only begun to understand what has happened to noetic processes in the long historical movement from primary orality to our present world. Much more remains to be done, and not only among psychoanalytic and other structuralists or among linguistic theorists. Even anthropologists, led by Jeffrey Opland and a few others, are only beginning to incorporate the Parry-Lord-Havelock findings into their work, though already the excitement here is high and growing. It might soon be even higher in the vast and carefully worked field of biblical studies, once it gets under way there. Scripture scholars have for some time been quite aware of the varied oral backgrounds of the books in the Bible, but thus far have shown little awareness of the psychodynamics of oral cultures—an awareness absolutely essential if understanding of the evolving noetic structures in the Bible is to have phenomenological depth relevant to our times. The American scholar Herbert N. Schneidau, not himself primarily a biblical specialist, has recently made the point that the kerygma itself of the Old Testament and of the New would have been impossible to realize in a primary oral culture untouched by writing, where total uncritical assimilation of individuals to their culture, such as Havelock has described in Homeric Greece, would have left no possibility for the newness and unsettling urgency of the biblical word. This means that adequate understanding of Judaism and of Christianity will have to come to grips with a phenomenology and depth psychology of writing as contrasted with antecedent primary orality. Among biblical scholars now grappling with the issues here the leader is Werner H. Kelber, in his pioneering work on Mark.

It has long been a commonplace that the use of language is distinctive of man. But only of late have we become more fully aware of the complexities such a commonplace involves. Language grows out of consciousness—naturally, for every conscious human being, unless physically or psychologically impaired, inevitably learns to speak. Through thought and language, humans assimilate the external world, as well as the interior world, to themselves in the sense that they come to know it and to a degree to understand it. But they assimilate it also in another and more mysterious way. They learn to use the physical products of the external world to build new possibilities into consciousness itself. Consciousness sacramentalizes the material world in many ways. One way is by building into this world its own transmaterial activities through writing and print and electronic technologies. As consciousness penetrates the material world, so this material world, through that organization that we call technology, bestowed on it by consciousness, penetrates consciousness too, where it not only takes on meaning but also implements the discovery of meaning, and thereby of the sacral itself.

Technology thus shows itself as something profoundly interior. The human word is at its origin an oral phenomenon and it remains, despite the grammatologies of antiquity, the Middle Ages, the Renaissance, the Enlightenment, and the twentieth century, irrevocably oral at root. All real words are spoken words. The marks on pages that we call words are of themselves verbal nothings that become real words only in the consciousness of real readers who process them, in however complexly coded fashions, through the world of sound. Yet the evolution of consciousness demands that the originally oral human word be distanced from orality, be technologized, reduced to writing and print and ultimately to computers, where it can be fed back into the oral world again.

A dialectic is at work here in this technologizing of the word. As has been noted earlier, a primary oral culture cannot describe the features of orality or reflect on itself as a culture. The very concept of culture is a typographically formed concept, dependent on the feel for a mass of knowledge that cannot be accumulated even with writing, but demands print. There is no way short of a massive descriptive circumlocution even to speak or think of "culture" in classical Latin. Only those advantaged by the interiorization of writing and print, and living at the opening of the electronic age, have been able to discover what primary orality was or is and to reflect on it and understand it, and thereby to reflect on manuscript cultures and typographic cultures and their own electronic culture itself. Locked in a primary oral culture, consciousness has not the kind of self-knowledge and hence not the freedom that only technology can confer when consciousness makes technology its own. Like human beings themselves as they pass through the successive phases of life and through their physical death, the oral word in a way must die too, if it is to bear fruit; that is, it must lose itself in writing and print and now in electronics, and in the interaction of all those technologies, if it is to realize its promise.

St. Louis University

Bibliography

Authors referred to in passing and not listed here are discussed either in the books here listed or in the references given in these books.

Biebuyck, Daniel, and Kahombo C. Mateene, editors and translators. *The Mwindo Epic: From the Banyanga*, as delivered by Candi Rureke. Berkeley and Los Angeles: University of California Press, 1971.

Culler, Jonathan. *Structuralist Poetics: Structuralism, Linguistics, and the Study of Literature*. Ithaca, N.Y.: Cornell University Press, 1975.

Derrida, Jacques. *De la Grammatologie*. Paris: Editions de Minuit, 1967.

————. *Of Grammatology*. Translated by Gayatri Chakravorty Spivak. Baltimore: The Johns Hopkins University Press, 1976.

Dundes, Alan. "The Making and Breaking of Friendship as a Structural Frame in African Folk Tales." In Pierre Maranda and Elli Köngas, eds., *Structural Analysis of Oral Tradition*. University of Pennsylvania Publications in Folklore and Folklife, No. 3. Philadelphia: University of Pennsylvania Press, 1971. Pp. 171–84.

Eccles, John C. "The Human Person." In *Conference Fabricated Man III: Brain Research-Human Consciousness*. St. Louis: Institute for Theological Encounter with Science and Technology, St. Louis University, 1975. Pp. 1–14, with discussion, pp. 15–22.

————. *The Understanding of the Brain*. New York: McGraw-Hill, 1973.

Gerbner, George, and Larry Gross. "Living with Television: The Violence Profile," *Journal of Communication* 26 (1976): 173–99.

Havelock, Eric A. *Preface to Plato*. Cambridge, Mass.: Harvard University Press, Belknap Press, 1963.

Kahler, Erich. *The Inward Turn of Narrative*. Translated by Richard and Clara Winston. Princeton: Princeton University Press, 1973.

Lord, Albert B. *The Singer of Tales*. Harvard Studies in Comparative Literature, 24. Cambridge, Mass.: Harvard University Press, 1960.

Manuel, Frank E. *The Religion of Isaac Newton*. Oxford: At the Clarendon Press, 1974.

Ong, Walter J. *Interfaces of the Word: Studies in the Evolution of Consciousness and Culture*. Ithaca: Cornell University Press, 1977.

————. *The Presence of the Word*. The Terry Lectures. New Haven: Yale University Press, 1967.

_____. *Ramus, Method, and the Decay of Dialogue*. Cambridge, Mass.: Harvard University Press, 1958.

_____. *Rhetoric, Romance, and Technology*. Ithaca: Cornell University Press, 1971.

Parry, Milman. *The Making of Homeric Verse: The Collected Papers of Milman Parry*. New York: Oxford University Press, 1971.

Pribram, Karl H. "A Neo-Cartesian Approach to the Mind-Body Relationship." In *Conference Fabricated Man III: Brain Research-Human Consciousness*. St. Louis: Institute for Theological Encounter with Science and Technology, St. Louis University, 1975. Pp. 23–44, with discussion, pp. 45–61.

Schneidau, Herbert N. *Sacred Discontent: The Bible and Western Tradition*. Berkeley and Los Angeles: University of California Press, 1977.

Weiss, Paul A. *Life, Order, and Understanding: A Theme in Three Variations*. Supplement to *The Graduate Journal*, vol. 7. Austin, Texas: The University of Texas Press, 1970.

Wilden, Anthony. *System and Structure: Essays in Communication and Exchange*. London: Tavistock Publications, 1972.

Index